Do prophets exist today? Ephesians chapter 4 lists prophets right alongside pastors, "for the edification of the body of Christ." For it is written, "believe His prophets, and you shall prosper." (2 Chron. 20:20) Often in the Bible the role of the prophet concerns that which is yet future. They sought the counsel of the prophet because he claimed to receive a fresh "rhema" word from the Lord for their particular situation. It is that still, small voice from the Spirit of the Living God. But how do we know the word is really from the Lord?

In the Bible we find both false prophets as well as true prophets. We are to test the spirits, whether they be from God. (1 John 4:1) A true prophet, unlike Hananiah, will never contradict the precepts of God. (Jer. 28)

"In the beginning was the Word (logos), and the Word was with God, and the Word was God." (John 1:1) The fresh rhema word spoken by a true prophet confirms and stirs up the Word, or logos, of God in our lives.

This is how we discern between a true and false prophet. Concerning these last days in which we are living, we are not to listen to false prophets. "Thus says the LORD of hosts: Do not listen to the words of the prophets...They continually say...'You shall have peace', and...'No evil shall come upon you.'...In the latter days you will understand it perfectly." (Jer. 23:17-20)

Many false prophets have been sent out into the world but there stands today, like a beacon in the dark of night, God's true prophets. As soon as I began reading Glynda's words, I knew they were straight from the Lord of Hosts. Many of her rhema words resonate what I had already been studying in the Bible concerning the last days, especially as it concerns God's people in America today.

I encourage everyone to study the Word of God and use it to validate the authenticity of Glynda's fresh rhema words from the Lord. You will be greatly blessed, as I have been, as you believe this true servant of God and benefit from her time spent in the presence of the Father.

Drew Simmons, Author of "Quenched Like a Wick",
(http://wakeupbabylon.blogspot.com)

Glynda Lomax and her ministry WINGS OF PROPHECY remind me all over again, that Jesus did not come to bring us a religion. Jesus came to introduce us to His Father, and to show and teach us that God wants us to have and enjoy an intimate, personal, trusting relationship with the God of all creation. America has been blessed as the crown of all nations in the world (with the exception of Israel). This crown is about to be removed as a sign of judgment from God unless America returns to her first love – the God of all creation. Glynda walks in submission and trust of the Lord Jesus Christ and willing to be led by His Holy Spirit, allows Glynda to hear from the Lord in a clear and unmistakable fashion, and the Lord is relaying to Glynda and WINGS OF PROPHECY His admonishment and His directions that a nations' spiritual problems cannot be solved by physical or monetary means, nor by man's wisdom of self-governance. The prophetic words delivered by this ministry are calling all who have ears to hear to prepare for God's direct discipline and judgment on this Nation who once could say, "Blessed is the Nation whose God is the Lord" (Ps. 33:12).

LYLE J. RAPACKI, Ph.D.
SENTINEL INTELLIGENCE SERVICES, LLC
Protective Intelligence and Assessment Specialist
Consultant on Behavioral Analysis and Threat Assessment
Private-Sector Intelligence Analyst

To all reading this book, you will be blessed mightily by Glynda's inspirational, sometimes alarming words from the Lord. She is graced by our merciful Father to hear His voice. For Christians not given this gift, we depend on those who are. Most importantly, it is vital that those who claim to hear His messages are trustworthy, humble, walk in The Word and only wish to serve. These are the very words that describe Glynda Lomax.

For several years we've posted on our website the Lord's warnings, encouragements and teachings via Glynda's Wings of Prophecy. Sometimes the message raise us up, sometimes they admonish His children, always they encourage us to seek His face, ask forgiveness and be thankful that the Gospel has been revealed through her ministry. His words are made even more vital, more pertinent through Glynda's sharings. Without question, we are in End Times and it is imperative that we hear His voice through scripture and His most obedient servants. In Glynda Lomax, you are gifted with these insights. Maranatha! - - *Holly Deyo (http://www.standeyo.com)*

For those awakening to the realization that the End of Days is nearly upon us, the Words that come through Glynda Lomax cannot be ignored. For those already awakened, they will shake you out of complacency and remind you what really matters in the times ahead.

The warnings revealed in this collection of messages are well worth heeding. Though they foretell of unprecedented challenging times fast approaching, there is another core message at the heart of all of them – draw close to God now and learn to receive His guidance, because that may be all we are left with in the days to come, despite our best efforts to be prepared. It's the ultimate advice for preppers, and it might save more than just your life...

Glynda Lomax is a source worthy of trust. Here is a woman who has given up her entire worldly life, midstream – everything – to answer the call to follow God, wherever that leads. Humble in spirit yet mighty in faith, her message is never about herself, and always about getting your life right with God, right now, in tangible and practical ways that may surprise you as well as awaken you. Read her books, watch her videos, listen to her radiocasts and be transformed. - *Scott L. Bach, Esq.*

Thank God that the Lord could find someone out there willing to pay the price, endure the suffering and stick with it long enough to hear God's Voice and to accurately relay the information that God has for His people in this late hour. For over a year now, my wife and I have looked forward to reading fresh and new words that God gives to His daughter Glynda, a True Woman of God and fellow laborer in the Lord's Work.

Brother Steven Millhorn
Radio Bible Teacher of Expounder Ministries
(http://www.expounderministries.com)

The Spirit of the Lord confirms His Word out of the mouths of two or three witnesses. I have noticed that when God is speaking certain ministries will perceive it and be faithful to reveal it. Wings OF Prophecy is one of those ministries.

I am often amazed when a word Glynda has received from the Lord either comes to pass or is confirmed by more witnesses. This is exciting! We can be confident that God still speaks today!

In "Wings of Prophecy", you will find a compilation of Words from the Lord that is relevant to people as individuals. Often what God says is very pertinent to what is going on in our individual lives. The Lord has touched me often on a personal note through the words Glynda has received. I have frequently received keys that have unlocked some of my personal dilemmas in my walk with the Lord.

In "Wings of Prophecy", many words are pertinent to nations as well. I am thankful that God is faithful to reveal His plan before hand. Amo 3:7 Surely the Lord GOD will do nothing, but he revealeth his secret unto his servants the prophets.

In a dark place, it is wise to bring a flashlight so that we can see how to walk. In "Wings of Prophecy" , the Word of God lights the way so we can see how to walk in the present and surge ahead into the future.

Conrad Carriker
Author of Open Your Eyes - My Supernatural Journey
(www.conradrocks.net)

The refreshing waves of sincerity and truth shine through in this prophetic album of end time events. The Holy Spirit has apprehended certain vessels throughout the last two thousand years of the Church Age to be a witness and testimony to His dealings with His people and with the world at large. This book is a compilation of the VOICE OF MANY WATERS speaking to a generation that might very well be on the one hand The Generation of His Wrath, while on the other hand The Generation of the Upright.

Sister Lomax has leaned close to the heart of her Messiah and has heard a word from His lips. She has undertaken the task of writing those words and sending them forth to the ends of the earth, that those who read them might run and prepare for the days of adversity, anguish, greatness, and glory!

It has been an awesome privilege to have had a part in not only reading them at a personal level, but also reading many of these words over the airwaves to over 57 nations around the world.

They are there! The people who have ears to hear are listening and allowing the grace of the Holy Spirit to take these prophetic words and guide these people into their safe haven where peace may be found yet still.

Take the time to listen, pray, and obey the words that are written in this book. Meditate on them and allow the penetrating power of the Holy Spirit to sanctify your soul at the deepest levels. Let the light shine through into your hearts and allow for the conviction of the Spirit to cause us once again to blush at those things that are an offense to God. Then let us rise from the brokenness of having fallen upon the ROCK and soar to new heights of divine glory as overcomers living in these last moments of time on earth as we know it.

I am thankful to Sister Lomax for allowing Jesus, who is the Spirit of Prophecy, to have such a large place in her life, allowing for the words of truth that have been marinated in the anointing to fill the hearts of the faithful with hope, faith, and love.

Pastor Vincent Xavier, New Wine Ministry Church
Bella Vista, Arkansas
(http://www.blogtalkradio.com/xman777)
newwineministry.net

Wings of Prophecy

FROM THE BEGINNING

A Compilation of Prophetic Messages and
Visions Received by Glynda Lomax

Edited by Rudolph C. Schafer

Wings of Prophecy - From the Beginning

By Glynda Lomax

See the author's latest at
http://wingsofprophecy.blogspot.com

Online videos available at
www.youtube.com/user/texasauthor1

Bi-weekly radio show at www.blogtalkradio.com/glyndalomax

International Standard Book Number
ISBN 13: 978-1477491577
ISBN 10: 1477491570

Editing contributed by Rudolph C. Schafer

Cover Design contributed by Jason Alexander, Lead Designer, www.ExpertSubjects.com

Scripture quotations from The Authorized (King James) Version. Rights in the Authorized Version in the United Kingdom are vested in the Crown. Reproduced by permission of the Crown's patentee, Cambridge University Press.

A liturgical work.

Printed in the United States of America

DEDICATION

To all my brothers and sisters in Christ. May the words
of our Lord strengthen, motivate and inspire you
through the rest of your journey here on earth.

ACKNOWLEDGEMENT

I would like to express my deep gratitude to my good friend, Rudolph C. Schafer who contributed his time and talent so *Wings of Prophecy - From the Beginning* could become a reality.

Thank you, Rudy. May God richly bless you for the many hours of prayer and editing you tirelessly sowed into this book.

PREFACE

The book you are about to read is from God. It is a collection of prophecies, visions, and revelations given by the Holy Spirit to Glynda Lomax—a spiritually sensitive, yielded vessel of the Lord. She received them during or just after times of prayer. A small number she received while doing routine activities. She would then record what God gave her in her prayer journal.

Before one would read a book like this, it must be understood that much of what is called "prophecy" or "the prophetic" in the Church today is not true Bible prophecy at all. A great deal of what passes for prophecy comes from the flesh—the carnal mind—and is not from the Holy Spirit at all. Other prophecies come from both the Holy Spirit and the flesh. This results in an impure mixture, an impure message. Some so-called words from God are given by unclean spirits, either partially or completely, thereby giving Satan direct entry into a church body. Still other prophecies do come from the Holy Spirit, but because of the spiritual condition and limitations of the receiving vessel are incomplete and shallow.

Some prophecies come from the Holy Spirit and are spiritually sound and complete but are intended for encouragement and comfort only, and nothing else. This is known as exhortation prophecy. It is common in the public assemblies of most Charismatic and Pentecostal churches, (as are the other types of prophecy mentioned in the previous paragraph). However, this type of prophecy is also shallow, and a constant, exclusive diet of this kind alone will never adequately feed a church body.

Unfortunately, in the overwhelming majority of Charismatic and Pentecostal churches in America today, this is usually the highest level of prophecy that ever comes forth, and even that level is reached just part of the time.

The last category, and the one that occurs the least but is needed by the church the most, is revelation prophecy. It requires a greater degree of yielding on the part of the person receiving the message. Revelation prophecy reveals more of the true heart and mind and nature of God—the riches of His depths and His ways, with nothing impure added and nothing pure missing. **Revelation prophecy teaches, guides, corrects, rebukes, nourishes, builds up, warns, and tells of things to come. <u>If heeded, it will totally transform a church or a people of God</u>.** That is the kind of prophecy that fills the pages of *Wings of Prophecy*, a book in which God is truly speaking to His people.

Rudolph C. Schafer

Compiler and Editor of *The Last Call* and *Prophecies of the End-Times*. The preceding Preface is an excerpt from these two books and was edited for *Wings of Prophecy - From the Beginning*.

Table of Contents

PREFACE...i

THE BLANKET OF DARKNESS 1

THE COMING ATTACK ON AMERICA 4

WEEP FOR AMERICA 5

THOSE WHO DO NOT MAKE TIME FOR GOD NOW.................... 8

THE ENEMY WILL PURSUE MY PEOPLE 9

THEY HAVE WORSHIPED OTHER GODS 11

FALSE SHEPHERDS WILL LOSE FLOCKS 12

THE GREAT WARRIORS 12

GREAT WARRIORS IN THE MIDST OF RAGING BATTLE 15

AWESOME WORSHIP?..16

CRY OUT TO ME FOR LOST LOVED ONES.................................16

GIVE TO THE PEOPLE ON THE STREETS 17

WHAT'S COMING IN 2011 19

LEAVE THE PAST BEHIND 21

GREAT CHANGE IS COMING - TRUST ME..................................22

OPEN YOUR HEARTS AND YOUR MINDS 24

THEY SHALL BE ASHAMED 25

AN EVENT IS COMING SOON THAT WILL SHOCK THE WORLD 27

A GREAT SAVING, HEALING, DELIVERING AND PSALMS MINISTRY IS COMING TO THIS NATION 29

A TIME OF MANY DANGERS 31

INCREASE IN WORDS RELEASED 33

AS YOU HAVE SOWN YOU WILL REAP 34

SUBMIT TO ME...37

MY CHOSEN ONES 38

THIS IS THE CALM BEFORE THE STORM 39

VIOLENT UPHEAVALS COMING 41

OBEY ME NOW 42

AMERICA WILL SUFFER MANY WOUNDS 45

A YEAR OF MUCH CHANGE 46

THE TIME OF MY GREAT WARRIORS 50

YOU HAVE HEARD THE WARNING SOUND 55

YOUR TIME HAS COME 57

DECLARE UNTO ME NOW 58

TROUBLE COMING 60

SITUATIONS NOT AS THEY APPEAR 63

THIS STORM WILL COME UPON YOU QUICKLY.................66

YOU CANNOT LOVE THE WORLD AND LOVE ME 69

DESTRUCTION IS COMING TO AMERICA 72

AMERICA HAS BECOME THE HARLOT OF THE WORLD.......75

I DESIRE MY PEOPLE WOULD PREPARE 77

WHEN WILL YOU HEED MY WORDS? 77

THERE SHALL BE WEEPING AND MOURNING IN AMERICA 81

I AM RAISING UP SOME OF YOU TO LEAD THE WAY 84

REPENT WHILE THERE IS STILL TIME 86

LET THE DIVIDING LINES BE DRAWN................................87

WHY DO YOU SAY YOU ARE MINE?..................................89

REND YOUR HEARTS TO ME 91

IT IS TIME TO CHOOSE 93

RISE UP AND FIGHT THE ENEMY 95

WHY DO YOU NOT WORSHIP ME?...................................97

AMERICA SHALL BOW 99

I DELIGHT IN YOUR TRUE WORSHIP OF ME 100

DRAW NEAR TO ME NOW 102

MY BRIDE IS INDIFFERENT TO ME 103

I WILL SHOWER THEM IN THE MIRACULOUS 106

YOU MUST FORGIVE..108

HARD TIMES LIE AHEAD..110

I AM COMING TO EVERY HOUSEHOLD 111

THE ENEMY HAS LULLED YOU TO SLEEP...................................113

I AM CALLING MY SOLDIERS TO WAR 114

DRAW NEAR TO ME...115

PREPARE YOUR HEARTS FOR WHAT I AM ABOUT TO DO 116

IT WILL BE A TIME AS NONE BEFORE IT.....................................117

CRY OUT TO ME 119

YOU MUST NOW CONSTANTLY SEEK MY FACE 120

MY PEOPLE MUST TAKE CONTROL OF THEIR MOUTHS 122

I WILL NOT LOOK THE OTHER WAY..123

THE TIME OF MY JUDGMENTS HAS COME 124

THIS SHALL BE A YEAR OF TURNING 125

SO WILL IT BE FOR EVERY NATION THAT FORGETS ME..................129

WHY IS YOUR FAITH SO SMALL? 131

ONLY ONE 132

BE VIGILANT...136

THE DAYS GROW DARKER STILL 138

CHANGE IS COMING..140

GREAT CHANGES...143

IT IS TIME 145

THEY SHALL BE DECEIVED...147

RESPONSE TO INQUIRIES ABOUT ATTACKS 148

A SAD TIME IS APPROACHING 149

SHE HAS TURNED AGAINST ME 151

HIS ATTACKS HAVE INCREASED 152

THE TIME OF SHAKING IS UPON YOU.............................153

THE TIME HAS COME TO PROMOTE MY PEOPLE..............155

WHICH IS MORE IMPORTANT? 157

YOU ARE TO BE THAT LIGHT 158

2012 - MANY CHANGES, MIRACLES 160

VISION OF THE WOUNDED LAMBS 163

BE NOT PUFFED UP 166

WHY DO YOU PLAY STILL? 168

SEEK ME FOR I SHALL BE FOUND 169

I WILL GIVE YOU THE KEYS...171

I AM STIRRING UP NATIONS 173

THE MEAT GRINDER VISION 175

A THROWAWAY GOD 177

THIS YEAR 178

WANT OF GAIN 181

UNIONS NOT OF ME...183

THE SHAKING IS BEGINNING......................................184

RELEASE WHAT IS NO LONGER USEFUL 186

PREPARE FOR WAR 187

A TIME OF MANY TRANSITIONS...................................189

CHAINED 192

AMERICA, AMERICA 194

CHANGE OF SEASONS...195

WILL YOU DENY ME? 196

THE NEW AGE IS BEGINNING......................................197

REGRET OR REWARD 199

SEEK WISDOM..202

AMERICA HAS BECOME A FESTERING WOUND 204

I DESIRE YOUR LOVE 207

I AM HE WHO DELIVERS 209

FORTIFY YOURSELVES..210

EPILOGUE..213

WEBSITES..216

CROSS REFERENCE INDEX BY SUBJECT 217

NOTES...228

THE BLANKET OF DARKNESS

(Vision January 17, 2008)

I was going back over my records of what the Lord has spoken to me over the past several years when I came across something He said on March 25, 2008, after He had shown me a vision during my worship time of a giant black blanket descending silently towards the earth. It was falling through space, and when I saw it, I got a really bad feeling. I did not understand what it meant at the time and had inquired of Him to reveal it to me.

The blanket of darkness you saw descending is spiritual blindness that is about to cover the earth. The people who have denied Me, those who have treated My Son's blood frivolously, those who do not walk in My ways, will be trapped in it. They will become prey to the Evil One and will be given over to their sinful ways. Their lusts shall consume them, and death shall be their reward

You are seeing My judgment fall on some already, but you will see this increase as the days pass, as I remove the blemishes that have shamed My Holy Name and profaned My church.

I will no longer look the other way from their sin but, I will uncover it for all the world to see. Disgrace shall be their reward. I will no longer tolerate sin in the church.

And the pretenders I shall also remove, for they are not of Me; they are not branches of the true vine. They sit like puppets, week after week, but their eyes do not see and their ears do not hear. They seek Me not and have aroused My holy anger.

My holy apostles and prophets I will send, and they will be run out as I shine the glorious light of My holiness on them. I shall drive all darkness from the bride of My Son!

Isaiah 60:2: For, behold, the darkness shall cover the earth, and gross darkness the people: but the LORD shall arise upon thee, and his glory shall be seen upon thee.

Galatians 5:24: And they that are Christ's have crucified the flesh with the affections and lusts.

Ephesians 2:3: Among whom also we all had our conversation in times past in the lusts of our flesh, fulfilling the desires of the flesh and of the mind; and were by nature the children of wrath, even as others.

VISIONS OF FAMINE COMING TO AMERICA

It was the evening of December 1, 2008 when the first vision came. I had just placed a bowl of beans into my microwave and pressed Start. Suddenly, it was as if a powerful wall of wind slammed into me and I no longer felt my body or knew anything about where I was. *I was looking down into a big soup pot and could smell beans, but what was in the pot was almost all water. I could feel famine all around and people starving to death along with their children. I saw bare cupboards, nothing in them but one or two spices.*

I was standing up when this vision came, and it was so powerful it almost knocked me to my knees. In the past, most of the visions I have had came during worship when I was already on my knees, but in the past year, I have begun to have more and more open visions when I am standing, just going about my daily routine.

The night after I was shown the first vision, I was sitting on my couch when the next visions came. *I saw people in the streets cooking over open fires in pots. What they were cooking smelled horrible, and yet they were so excited just to have anything at all to eat. Their eyes were wild with hunger. I saw great, open sores on the children. I didn't see any small children at all. These were all probably 11 years old or older, but they were covered in large, open sores. They all wore old, ragged clothing, and the sky was gray. It seemed to be cold outside.*

I looked into one woman's eyes and saw a combination of desperation and madness. She was cooking in one of the pots, and somehow I knew she was cooking the entrails of a dog. She was so happy to have something to eat, though the smell coming from that pot would not make you think it was anything you would eat at all. I saw no live animals in my vision, and I sensed they had almost all died from starvation already or people had caught them and eaten them.

I saw people dropping in the street and just dying there from starvation. Others just walked past them. They were all kind of scuffling along like they were in shock. No vehicles were on the road, no one was driving. I could also sense that there was no "entertainment" (television, etc.) going on anywhere.

There was terrible desperation in the eyes of those begging people. It was heartbreaking to look at. America, once so plentiful, was reduced to third world country status. People starving and dying in the streets—like what we hear happens in Africa. I felt helpless to save them.

Father, why am I being shown such terrible things?

Tell My people, daughter. Warn My people this is coming so they can prepare and be ready! Tell them I said to get ready to help those who are unsaved, for the end is very near now. Tell them to cling not to their own lives, but be willing to lay them down for a higher glory, for MY glory! Tell them to give all, even when they themselves are in need; for many will die and go to

Hell in that time, and those left behind will experience a fate even worse than that.

The Beast, the False Prophet—all that was foretold in Revelations—is about to come true. FEAR NOT THEIR FACES, FOR I WILL PROTECT YOU. Tell them, My child, tell them, though you know many will not listen. Many hard hearted ones will perish in that time but others will listen. I will open the hearts of those who have ears to hear and those who are being interceded for. Tell My people I said to pray diligently for those you love, so they will not be lost in that time; FOR MANY WILL WANT TO TAKE THE MARK OF THE BEAST, AND IF THEY DO THERE IS NO TURNING BACK FOR THEM. Tell them!

Ezek. 14:12-13: The Word of the LORD came again to me, saying . . . when the land sinneth against me by trespassing grievously, then will I stretch out mine hand upon it, and will break the staff of the bread thereof, and will send famine upon it, and will cut off man and beast from it:

THE COMING ATTACK ON AMERICA

Not long after the famine visions in early December 2008, I had another vision. This one was of a nuclear attack.

I knew in the Spirit I was in an American city, but I did not see the skyline, and I had no feeling about which one it was. It was a pretty tall skyscraper, probably at least 30-40 stories high.

This was an open vision, and when it opened up before me, I was looking at a skyscraper. I was taken in the Spirit close to one of the windows up high, and I could see there was a party or celebration of some sort going on inside.

I saw a woman with dark hair pinned up, dressed in a long blue sequin dress, and a man in a suit talking to her. Many people were around them at the party, and they were all talking.

Then I looked up, and over the building I saw a nuclear missile headed directly for the building. I don't know what city it was in, but it was completely dark in the vision, so I knew it was happening at night. It was obvious no one at the party had even the slightest clue the attack was coming.

I know others who are unbelievers who for the last eight or nine years have been having visions of nuclear attacks on America. The visions are always the same, and they come like nightmares to them. (I believe God is warning even His chosen, who do not yet know they are chosen.) In some of the visions, the attack is on a specific city, and the vision is of an airplane falling from the sky. Another person has repeated visions of complete devastation from multiple attacks in numerous cities (3-6) across America that happen almost simultaneously. These seers have also seen the famine that is coming.

WEEP FOR AMERICA

April 1, 2009

I was praying and asking God to help me distance myself from distractions so that I could be more effective in my time in His Word and in prayer when He spoke this to me.

The world around you is filled with distractions. Many of My children do not spend time with Me at all, but the cost to them will be great in the days coming, FOR I SHALL POUR OUT MY JUDGMENT UPON ALL THOSE WHO DO NOT SEEK TO KNOW ME OR MY WILL FOR THEIR LIVES. No longer shall I look on as they go their own way, following their own plans, but I will smite them with a curse until they turn their faces to Me in repentance!

The days are quickly approaching when gross darkness shall cover the earth, and men's hearts shall be darkened. No more will they be able to turn to Me and choose My way, for they will have worshiped their own way, and I shall give them the fruits of it.

THIS NATION IS NO LONGER UNDER MY BLESSING BUT UNDER A CURSE, and those who have not chosen to know Me will soon feel My Hand of Judgment heavy upon them. Cry, My children! Cry out for those you love! Weep and wail, mourn for the unrepentant hearts, for souls are at stake! Cry out to Me for mercy for them, for I am the only One who can save them from the flames of eternal damnation!

Weep and wail for this lost nation, for soon it shall drink from the cup of bitterness as I have ordained! Weep for it! Cry out for the unsaved, for many shall perish in that hour! My fire falls on those who love Me and serve Me, but a different fire is coming for the wicked, and they know it not! I hold My own in the palm of My mighty hand to protect them, but I shall pour out My anger on the wicked and unrepentant, and My judgments are coming soon!

Cry, My children! Cry and mourn in travail for the lost, for this is My heart!

Why waste ye hours praying over building funds and music programs while the hungry and lost walk in darkness? Did Jesus build buildings? Did He run music programs? Nay! He fed the hungry, visited those who were sick and healed them, He prayed and taught unbelievers, He called sinners to repentance!

Why do I see My precious widows and orphans sitting alone while My shepherds and priests meet each other daily over expensive lunches? I say those who do not repent of this before Me with tears will pay a grave price! You seek to build your own *houses and ignore Mine! I shall tear your idols from your hands and leave you weeping with no places of worship for forsaking Me, the Fount of Living Water! I shall leave your little ones fatherless and crying in the streets for bread when I smite you with a curse!*

Weep and howl for your sins have come up before Me, and they are grievous! Weep and howl for the fates that await your young ones for your lack of obedience and unrepentant hearts! Weep for your nation, for she has forsaken Me, and now she must be judged; and you will stand in awe of My mighty power as My Hand of Judgment moves against her!

I will strike her with fire, with famine, and disease! The screams of the wicked I will not hear in that time. I will give her enemies power to burn her and torture her. They will spoil her riches and ruin her beauty because she has forsaken Me and My ways! No more shall she be called the land of the free and the blessed, but she shall be termed desolate—jackals shall lodge where her cities once stood so proudly. Weeds will cover her, and insects will feed on the flesh of the dead in her streets.

Then will you know that I AM the Lord your God and Me only shall you serve and worship!

Jeremiah 25:36-38: A voice of the cry of the shepherds, and an howling of the principal of the flock, shall be heard: for the LORD hath spoiled their pasture. And the peaceable habitations are cut down because of the fierce anger of the LORD. He hath forsaken his covert, as the lion: for their land is desolate because of the fierceness of the oppressor, and because of his fierce anger.

April 3, 2009

THOSE WHO DO NOT MAKE TIME FOR GOD NOW

I was praying Friday night, April 3rd, 2009, and I inquired of God why so many people tell me they do not hear Him speak.

Why do others not hear You, Lord? I know You want to talk to them. Why can I hear You but so many of them say they don't? I know I am no one special.

It depends on how many things they put before Me in their lives.

In my spirit I saw a large room. I saw Jesus on one end and a person who believed in Him on the other. Many, many things were between Jesus and the person I saw. I saw Him trying to tell the person something, but His gentle voice could not be heard over all the space and clutter that separated them. They were preoccupied with all the things. He was way down on their lists, though this person professed to know and serve Him. I saw in the Spirit that their service consisted of motions, for none of their time was His. I saw it belonged instead to their employers, their families, their educational pursuits, and their goals and ambitions to succeed in this life. I was given this same vision twice.

To all these things give they their time. They have no time for Me—the One who created them and gave them life. And in that terrible Day of Judgment coming soon, I will not hear their cries—not for them nor for their loved ones.

Warn My people, child! Tell them IF THEY DO NOT MAKE TIME FOR ME NOW AND REVERENCE ME AS ALMIGHTY GOD, THAT I WILL ANSWER NOT THEIR CRIES IN THEIR HOUR OF NEED! I require more than mere words as their service to Me! I require their hearts to be Mine also! I require first position in their lives, not to be relegated to last like some servant they have no time for. I will have first place in their hearts!

They languish in the many blessings I have given them, and acknowledge Me, not by servicing those I have called them to. Therefore I will remove the blessings from them in one day—they will seek Me then!

Jer. 11:11+13: Therefore thus saith the LORD, Behold, I will bring evil upon them, which they shall not be able to escape; and though they shall cry unto me, I will not hearken unto them. For according to the number of thy cities were thy gods, O Judah; and according to the number of the streets of Jerusalem have ye set up altars to that shameful thing,

THE ENEMY WILL PURSUE MY PEOPLE

April 24, 2009

Yea, a time is coming to My people when the enemy will pursue them so closely that they will feel his hot breath on the backs of their necks, saith the Lord—a time when none shall be sure what to do. All will fear, and many will die in their astonishment as My mighty Hand of Judgment moves against a people hard hearted and wicked in their ways before Me, saith the Lord of Hosts.

This people has not turned to Me, but away from Me and done their own good pleasure and not Mine, saith the Lord. Yes, and I will give them the fruits of their doings. I will give to them the reward of the wicked. For the wages of sin is always death. Death and destruction will come in the night to those who do not fear Me nor My Holy Name, saith the Holy One of Israel. Nothing will be strong enough to save them from My mighty power, for none are stronger than Me, saith the Lord.

I have warned them. I have sent My prophets to announce My displeasure with their wicked ways, to warn them of what was to come, but few have listened and fewer turned back from their ways.

Darkness comes to this nation now, a dark time, dark hours that will stretch endlessly before it, for its wickedness is great and has come up before Me.

Where are My intercessors? Where are My prayer warriors? Where are My anointed children whom I have called for such a time as this? Why are they not weeping and travailing before Me for this nation? Why do they not cry out to Me, Abba, for salvation for the lost? Why do they go on about their merry way, ignoring Me until they need something from Me?

I say to you that they shall not find Me in their hour of need. Many shall say "Lord, Lord," but I never knew them; and My Spirit will not save them in that hour if they do not turn to Me now.

My patience has grown thin, and I have grown weary with this prideful people who say they are Mine but do not act like Me.

Jer. 7: 20 23 24: Therefore thus saith the LORD God; Behold, mine anger and my fury shall be poured out upon this place, upon man, and upon beast, and upon the trees of the field, and upon the fruit of the ground; and it shall burn, and not be quenched. But this thing commanded I them, saying, Obey my voice, and I will be your God, and ye shall be my people: and walk ye in all the ways that I have commanded you, that it may be well unto you. But they hearkened not, nor inclined their ear, but walked in the counsels and in the imagination of their evil heart, and went backward, and not forward.

Matt. 7:21-23: Not every one that saith unto me, Lord, Lord, shall enter into the kingdom of heaven; but he that doeth the will of my Father which is in heaven. Many will say to me in that day, Lord, Lord, have we not prophesied in thy name? and in thy name have cast out devils? And in thy name done many wonderful works? And then I will profess unto them, I never knew you: depart from me, ye that work iniquity.

THEY HAVE WORSHIPED OTHER GODS

I received this Word in May of 2009.

I always keep My promises, for I am a faithful and loving God, unlike the gods My people make of their paychecks, houses, and investment accounts. I shall surely show them they have worshiped gods which have neither power to save nor deliver them from the times to come when great darkness shall enfold this land.

The time for My bride to arise and shine is now. My bride shall walk in truth and in holiness, in love and honor to one another, and against all that is evil and not of Me.

Strive to enter in, My people! Strive to enter into this time of cleansing, of purging from My bride all that is not of Me, for I shall not receive those who fail to allow Me to purify them. Strive to enter in to the peace of rest in Me where you shall find rest for your souls.

My Word is absolute and there is no varying in Me. I judge in righteousness, in truth and in holiness.

Isaiah 60:2: For, behold, the darkness shall cover the earth, and gross darkness the people: but the LORD shall arise upon thee, and his glory shall be seen upon thee.

FALSE SHEPHERDS WILL LOSE FLOCKS

I received this Word sometime in the spring or summer of 2009.

The shepherds who call themselves by My Name who are not Mine will soon find themselves with no flock, for I shall take their flocks from them. Those who use My Mighty Name for profit and gain will lose the riches they worship instead of Me.

This is the time of My cleansing fire—I will have a pure and holy bride! All that is not holy I will deal with, and you are not to associate with such!

Jeremiah 25:34-38: Howl, ye shepherds, and cry; and wallow yourselves in the ashes, ye principal of the flock: for the days of your slaughter and of your dispersions are accomplished; and ye shall fall like a pleasant vessel. And the shepherds shall have no way to flee, nor the principal of the flock to escape. A voice of the cry of the shepherds, and an howling of the principal of the flock, shall be heard: for the LORD hath spoiled their pasture. And the peaceable habitations are cut down because of the fierce anger of the LORD. He hath forsaken his covert, as the lion: for their land is desolate because of the fierceness of the oppressor, and because of his fierce anger.

THE GREAT WARRIORS

July 14, 2009

I noticed many Christians around me seemed to be getting easily offended or getting "attitudes"—people who normally were humble and loving. After talking to friends who are also sold out to the Most High God and finding out that they too, were experiencing this, I approached the throne to inquire of God if some spirit had been released by the enemy or what we could do about the situation.

All of us have also been fighting discouragement and noticed our usual joy in the Lord was not present. We also have all been feeling very oppressed along with facing attacks and offended attitudes by Christian brothers and sisters. Our stories were so similar it was shocking.

As I began to pray and to worship, I heard:

Repair the breach.

I began to search the Scriptures for what exactly that means and found Isaiah 58:12: "And they that shall be of thee shall build the old waste places: Thou shalt raise up the foundations of many generations; and thou shalt be called, the repairer of the breach, the restorer of paths to dwell in." As I prayed and asked God what it meant, He began to speak a Word to me:

Go and repair the breach, My children! Build up, build up My church, My holy bride, for the final hour has come! March! March, form ranks, and FIGHT for MY CHURCH!

Lift up holy hands and pray for My children! Strengthen one another, for the battle rages around you in the realm you cannot see and soon will rage around you in the earth.

Few are truly prepared for this final hour—strengthen the ones I send to you, lift up the weak, shine as My light into dark places in this final hour! Pray for the lost and deceived, for soon they will no longer be able to choose My way over the world's.

Prepare ye for battle, My chosen ones! Prepare ye well, for the battle will be intense against you in this final hour! MY ANGELS ALSO FIGHT ALONG WITH YOU IN THE BATTLE. So fear not and cling not to your own lives, but be ready to lay them down for the lives of others who do not know Me yet, for they will face eternity in Hell if they choose not My way.

Soon it will end, My children. I will come and gather you to Myself, and this battle will be over. You will be here with Me in

Heaven. You will look upon the face of My Precious Son and never know sorrow again. Be strong for Me, children! Honor My Name in this final hour before you come home. Go! Go tell the others about Me that they may know Me before it is too late!

Gird up your loins! The battle will be fierce around you, and the worst has not yet begun. Cover the others in prayer that know Me not, and I shall save them, but do not stray from the narrow path, for other paths lead to destruction in this final hour.

I will strengthen you in coming days. I will visit some of you and manifest Myself to you. I will speak to you and tell you what you must do for My Name's sake. In these final days you shall see more of Me in the earth than ever before and also more of the enemy.

In my spirit I heard these words: *Opposing forces turning up the heat of the battle.*

My hand of protection covers you and protects you, until time for you to come home to Me. So do not be afraid, for I will sustain you in the midst of the evil that you may go forth declaring My Name, My glory, My saving power.

Zech. 10:5: And they shall be as mighty men, which tread down their enemies in the mire of the streets in the battle: and they shall fight, because the LORD is with them, and the riders on horses shall be confounded.

Matt. 7:13: Enter ye in at the straight gate: for wide is the gate, and broad is the way, that leadeth to destruction, and many there be which go in thereat:

Luke 10:19: Behold, I give unto you power to tread on serpents and scorpions, and over all the power of the enemy: and nothing by any means shall hurt you.

John 14:21: He that hath my commandments, and keepeth them, he it is that loveth me: . . . and I will love him, and will manifest myself to him.

GREAT WARRIORS IN THE MIDST OF RAGING BATTLE

As I continued to pray, a vision appeared in my spirit: *From high above I saw the earth with many people on it. I saw the enemy's people and I saw God's people. The enemy's people were fierce and very strong. They rushed God's people, and many of them fell in battle. Each time they rushed, more fell. It was like it came in thrusts. They were merciless against the people of God—an extremely violent force. I saw many fall in the first and second waves. It was obvious God's people were not ready for this battle. They fell easily—almost without a fight.*

But then I began to see just a few warriors in places across the area who were strengthened. They seemed to have a special strength and wisdom, and everywhere I saw them, I could see there was calm in their spirits. They had deadly determination against the enemy, but they were calm inside, unafraid. I felt in my spirit that they knew they would eventually lose their lives in the battle, but they were getting their instructions from On High, and God was sustaining them to go on and on—further and further—to accomplish His will and tell others during battle.

It was as if they were determined to do as much damage to the kingdom of darkness as possible before they went down. Many of them seemed alone, but they shone brighter and stronger than those around them. It was as if they were made of steel, and the look in their eyes was absolute. They were dressed for battle, and I knew in my spirit they were prepared for what lay ahead. It was obvious from their royal clothing that they fought for the King.

AWESOME WORSHIP?

Earlier, on July 14, 2009 while in prayer, *I saw in the Spirit a group of people worshiping at a church. The worship was awesome, and they all felt the presence of God in a mighty way. Then my viewpoint widened, and I saw that they were only on the very edge of His presence and that they were not actually seeking God, but they were seeking the "high" or feeling they got during worship. They were completely missing the One who brought the joy they felt. I could feel that this made the heart of our God very sad because He wants to be sought and known for who He is—The Most High God and a loving and merciful Father to us all.*

CRY OUT TO ME FOR LOST LOVED ONES

I was praying in the Spirit on September 21, 2009 when I received this Word:

This is what I desire of you—that you would spend your hours lying before Me in intercession. There I will reveal My glory to you. There I will reveal My truths to you. There I will tell you what to do as the days grow dark and this world approaches the end. It is there I desire My people to be—ever seeking My face; and to do My will, sharing My heart for the lost. For did I not send My only begotten Son for just that purpose—to save the lost, to bring them back to Me? It is here in My presence that you will find peace. It is here that you will experience Me. Here, crying out for those who do not know Me.

Lay aside the cares of this world, the thoughts about your needs. Did I not say in My Word to seek first My Kingdom, and all these things you need would be added unto you? Why then do you worry so for what you will wear or what you will eat? Am I not a wealthy Father, well able to provide all you need and more? Am I not able to take care of you, My little flock?

Stop wandering and wailing in the world, and focus on My purpose—to save the lost—and you will find your every need met in the earth and much, much more!

I am calling out to My intercessors: Fall on your faces and cry out to Me! Wail for your lost loved ones, for your unsaved families and friends, for the lost you do not know! Call on My Name, the only name that can save them from destructions to come! Cry out! Weep for them, My children, while there is yet time for them to be saved! There is no better use of your time. Come! Share My heart!

Isaiah 59:16: And he saw that there was no man, and wondered that there was no intercessor: therefore his arm brought salvation unto him; and his righteousness, it sustained him.

Job 42:10: And the LORD turned the captivity of Job, when he prayed for his friends: also the LORD gave Job twice as much as he had before.

1/01/11

GIVE TO THE PEOPLE ON THE STREETS

The Lord is beginning to move on the hearts of His people to reach out to the destitute and lonely more and to give more freely. Some of you have even been feeling the urge to sell some items you can do without so that you can give the money to feed the homeless or share with those who have nothing. God is saying to you:

Give, My people! Give to your brothers and sisters, to the people on the street. For when you give to them, you are giving to Me, and many of you are giving to angels unknowingly, and your reward shall be very great for doing so!

Give Me to them as well—in the form of My Word, My love, My compassion. Let the broken and hurting in this world see Me at work in you, reaching out to them; for in this way many shall come to know Me as their Lord and Savior. Be My hands and feet in a lost and dying world.

Many of you desire to be My voice, but secretly you seek your own glory and not Mine, and for this reason I cannot use you in that way. I desire My children to share with one another, and I will heap great and mighty blessings—so large they cannot be contained—on those who do this for My Name's sake.

You say you want to be blessed and yet you refuse to obey Me when I urge you to do something. Do you not realize the two go hand in hand? Do you not know blessing follows obedience?

Matthew 25:40: And the King shall answer and say unto them, Verily I say unto you,   Inasmuch as ye have done it unto one of the least of these my brethren, ye have done it unto me.

Luke 3:11: He answereth and saith unto them, He that hath two coats, let him impart to him that hath none; and he that hath meat, let him do likewise.

Luke 6:38: Give, and it shall be given unto you; good measure, pressed down, and shaken together, and running over, shall men give into your bosom. For with the same measure that ye mete withal it shall be measured to you again.

Deut. 15:11: For the poor shall never cease out of the land: therefore I command thee, saying, Thou shalt open thine hand wide unto thy brother, to thy poor, and to thy needy, in thy land.

Luke 12:33: Sell that ye have, and give alms; provide yourselves bags which wax not old, a treasure in the heavens that faileth not, where no thief approacheth, neither moth corrupteth.

1/01/11

WHAT'S COMING IN 2011

The Lord says, *I am beginning a new thing in your life, and I am going to do it in a new way. Expect something unexpected.*

I saw that the level of blessings you receive in 2011 will be in direct proportion to how much of yourself you have laid down for Him, His ways, and His Kingdom.

An abundance of blessings awaits you in this New Year that will be a great contrast to the lack of previous years.

Oh yes, I have promised you much and you say, "Where is it, Lord? Where yet is the fulfillment of all Your promises in my life?" Some of you wonder if you even truly heard from Me, so long has been the fulfillment in coming.

But I say to you now, ARISE, My people, and take your places! Arise, My great warriors whom I have trained in the hard times and dark places. Arise and take your places on the battlefield and fight for My glory! Fight for what you know is righteous! Fight against unrighteousness. Fight it first in yourself, then in your houses, your churches, and your schools.

The Lord showed me in my spirit a great need for integrity in His people. The Lord wants us to walk in integrity. He wants us to deal with wrong attitudes, behaviors, and relationships in our lives. I believe the Lord is saying He wants us to prune these things ourselves—not wait for Him to deal with us about it.

For I will have a holy people, and I am coming this year to burn out all that is not of Me in your life. Where there is corruption among you, I will expose it. I will leave no darkness unexposed, so repent now!

Wicked shepherds will I topple from the great pedestals to which they have exalted themselves, and I shall replace them with the humble—those who have continually humbled themselves before Me in prayer, in travail, and in intercession.

When the Lord spoke this to me, I saw a vision of Jesus over-turning the tables of the money changers. This is what the Lord is going to do this year. He is going to drive out what is crooked from His temple.

To those of you who call yourselves by My Name and continue to live lives of sin, I say this: "Prepare yourselves. Prepare to face My judgment in your life, for you shall indeed reap the fruit of your doings if you refuse to repent. Some of you will visit Hell this year, and SOME OF YOUR LIVES WILL FEEL LIKE YOU ARE THERE BECAUSE OF YOUR LACK OF REPENTANCE."

No longer shall I tolerate sin among My people, for I will have a holy bride! I will be God in your life if you are going to call Me your God! Do not speak vain, useless words.

I saw in my spirit, people who say "I'm a Christian, He's my God, " but the truth is He is not your God if you're not living like He's your God.

The time is quickly approaching when all must choose Me or the ways of the world. Even now battle lines are being drawn and peoples divided. Will you choose Me?

I saw more and more the unrighteous standing up and demanding their "rights," and I saw that increasingly in the future if you call yourself a Christian, the price you will have to pay is going to go up and up and up just for calling yourself by His name.

Jeremiah 17:10: I the LORD search the heart, I try the reins, even to give every man according to his ways, and according to the fruit of his doings.

Isaiah 43:18-19: Remember ye not the former things, neither consider the things of old. Behold, I will do a new thing; now it shall spring forth; shall ye not know it? I will even make a way in the wilderness, and rivers in the desert.

1/02/11

LEAVE THE PAST BEHIND

God is saying to His people: *Let go of the past My people, for there is now no time for looking back. And did I not say in My Word that he who sets his hands to the plough and looks back is not worthy of Me?*

I am moving you forward at an accelerated pace, and there is no time to waste on things that have already been—things you cannot change. Let go. Let go and let Me move you into all that I have for you.

This year will bring many changes into your lives, and some of those changes may not be positive in your eyes, but I shall work them all together for your good and for the good of My Kingdom. You must be standing ready to obey My every command if you are to be used in My Kingdom. You must throw off the grave clothes of your past and move forward in My anointing. Move forward, My people. Take your eyes off of what has been and can never be again. Loose the bands of pain from your past and let them go!

COMMAND THE ENEMY TO STOP TORMENTING YOUR MINDS WITH PAINFUL RECOLLECTIONS.

Luke 9:62: And Jesus said unto him, No man, having put his hand to the plough, and looking back, is fit for the kingdom of God.

Philippians 3:12: Not as though I had already attained, either were already perfect: but I follow after, if that I may apprehend that for which also I am apprehended of Christ Jesus.

Luke 5:36-39: And he spake also a parable unto them; No man putteth a piece of a new garment upon an old; if otherwise, then both the new maketh a rent, and the piece that was taken out of the new agreeth not with the old. And no man putteth new wine into old bottles; else the new wine will burst the bottles, and be spilled, and the bottles shall perish. But new wine must be put into new bottles; and both are preserved. No man also having drunk old wine straightway desireth new: for he saith, The old is better.

1/04/11

GREAT CHANGE IS COMING - TRUST ME

The Spirit of the Lord is saying, *If you will do My will and not your own, all the things I have shown you will surely come to pass. Do not fear the changes that are coming, for when you fear, you close the door on My blessings. For did I not say in My Word that without faith it is impossible to please Me? Therefore fear not, only believe.*

Many of you are coming into times of tremendous change in your life, and I say to you, put your hand in Mine and trust Me. Trust Me to lead you where you need to be as a small child trusts a parent. Trust Me that you will have enough even when it looks as if you will have nothing at all. Trust Me that My will for you is better than your own and My ways are higher than your ways. At times it will appear as if nothing is working out, but then you will see My hand move suddenly on your behalf and your needs will be met. Know that if you believe Me, you will see this often and learn not to believe the enemy's lies that I will not provide for you. Learn to trust Me completely, for I know what is best.

In times to come, many of you will be moving to other places, places you have not been to before. I say again, this is My hand—trust Me. Trust me to provide for you in strange lands, in unknown territories, in situations you have never faced before. Do not fear, only believe. You will face new and strange situations, but know this: I have gone before you to make the crooked places straight. I have gone before you and placed provisions along your path, and you will not be without as the enemy would have you to believe.

Many of you have stood in faith for years believing Me for a godly mate, and to you I say this: Your time is now! This year I will join many couples and ordain many to be together and work for Me. Be about your Father's business, for this is when I shall bring your mate to you, as you are both going about My business and doing My bidding.

Many visions shall be fulfilled this year, many prophecies come to pass. A time of great darkness is upon the earth, and sudden change will become common.

Hebrews 11:6: But without faith it is impossible to please him: for he that cometh to God must believe that he is, and that he is a rewarder of them that diligently seek him.

Genesis 15:1: After these things the Word of the LORD came unto Abram in a vision, saying, Fear not, Abram: I am thy shield, and thy exceeding great reward.

Isaiah 40:4: Every valley shall be exalted, and every mountain and hill shall be made low: and the crooked shall be made straight, and the rough places plain.

Isaiah 45:2: I will go before thee, and make the crooked places straight: I will break in pieces the gates of brass, and cut in sunder the bars of iron.

Isaiah 55:9: For as the heavens are higher than the earth, so are my ways higher than your ways, and my thoughts than your thoughts.

1/05/11

OPEN YOUR HEARTS AND YOUR MINDS

I am able to do so much more than My people are believing Me for! Open your hearts and your minds, My people, for I am a great and a Mighty God!

Do you think Me weak and unable like the gods you have made of your jobs, your paychecks, and your government? I am Jehovah! There is nothing too hard for Me.

Strive to have peace in the midst of your situation, for I am coming back soon; and I desire to find you watching, praying, and praising Me.

Open your minds and your hearts and allow Me to fully come in and change you.

Jer. 32:27: Behold, I am the LORD, the God of all flesh: is there anything too hard for me?

Rom. 12:2: And be not conformed to this world: but be ye transformed by the renewing of your mind, that ye may prove what is that good, and acceptable, and perfect, will of God.

1/06/11

THEY SHALL BE ASHAMED

The Spirit of the Lord is saying: *In times past there were those near you who mocked and rejected you because you heard My voice. Some walked away, so sure were they that you were only hearing from yourself. I say to you now that they shall be ashamed in times to come as I exalt you into all I have called you to be. I say to you now that you shall have double for the reproach you have born in silence for My Name's sake.*

Believe Me when I tell you that I shall repay in full and in double portion to all My children who have suffered rejection and mockery and persecution. In times to come when hardship abounds, you shall not suffer as they will suffer because you have known My Name, you have walked with Me and cried out to Me, you have lain in My presence and sought My face.

In times to come, you shall not do without, as those who mocked you and those who have mocked Me. Great will be your reward, and great shall be their punishment, and the contrast shall be made clear in what is coming. No more shall you walk in reproach, for I shall lift you up, says the Lord of Hosts.

I shall exalt you to all that I have called you to be, and you shall do without no good thing in that time, says the Lord. You shall walk in healing, in abundance, and in the joy of knowing your name is written in My Book of Life.

YOU SHALL WALK WITH A FIERY ANOINTING; AND MIRACLES, SIGNS, AND WONDERS SHALL ABOUND IN YOUR LIFE.

Do you not know that the fire had to burn first in your own life to remove all that was not of Me? Do you not know that I could not place the fire of My glory upon you until you were pure and strong enough to carry its power where I send you? Great will be the persecution of My people in days to come, but greater still shall be My power and My glory in the earth; and My people shall become as beams of light in the darkness of all that will be transpiring as the earth groans with the labor pains of My soon return.

Take heart, My children, for the time is short before you return home to Me to live forever in all I have prepared for you. Take heart and know I watch over you with great care every moment of your lives, and I see every situation you are in, and I care. Take heart in knowing it shall not be for much longer, and it will all be far more than worthwhile, no matter what the pain is you must bear in the meantime for Me. Be strong and courageous for My Name's sake. Be strong as you go forth and carry My Name to the ends of the earth and preach My glorious gospel to all peoples before My return.

Matt. 5:11-12: Blessed are ye, when men shall revile you, and persecute you, and shall say all manner of evil against you falsely, for my sake. Rejoice, and be exceeding glad: for great is your reward in heaven: for so persecuted they the prophets which were before you.

1 Tim. 4:10: For therefore we both labour and suffer reproach, because we trust in the living God, who is the Saviour of all men, specially of those that believe.

Isaiah 61:7: For your shame ye shall have double; and for confusion they shall rejoice in their portion: therefore in their land they shall possess the double: everlasting joy shall be unto them.

Psalm 104:4: Who maketh his angels spirits; his ministers a flaming fire.

Isaiah 10:16: Therefore shall the Lord, the Lord of hosts, send among his fat ones leanness; and under his glory he shall kindle a burning like the burning of a fire.

Joshua 1:9: Have not I commanded thee? Be strong and of a good courage; be not afraid, neither be thou dismayed: for the LORD thy God is with thee whithersoever thou goest.

1/13/11

AN EVENT IS COMING SOON THAT WILL SHOCK THE WORLD

The Lord told me that *this year will be intense.*

Great change is coming.

An event is coming soon that will shock the world. Great loss of life will be involved. There is nothing you can do to stop it from happening; it is already set. When it comes, My people, do not fear, but draw nearer to Me and I will instruct you what to do. Seek My peace and do not be afraid. You will want to run in terror, but there is nowhere for you to hide except in Me. And I tell you now that for those who truly walk with Me, those who truly are doing My will, not one hair on your heads will be harmed unless it is My time for you to be called home to Me.

Perilous times have come upon the earth and upon all My people.

I WILL BE SPEAKING SOON TO MANY OF MY PEOPLE TO FLEE THEIR PLACES, FOR DANGER IS COMING AND THEY KNOW IT NOT.

MY PEOPLE, A TIME OF WRATH IS SOON TO COME UPON THE EARTH. You will be both shocked and saddened as you see the events unfold that are coming. I speak to you now to prepare— prepare ye the way of the cross in your heart, for many of you will be sacrificed in that time. Prepare the way for lost sinners to receive My glorious gospel when they run to you in terror, for they will know nowhere else to turn. Prepare ye your hearts to walk in love in a time such as none that has come before it.

So many of My people are out playing the field, giving themselves to other gods, and they know not the hour is at hand when they will answer to Me. THEY HAVE BELIEVED THE ENEMY'S LIES THAT THEY WILL NOT BE JUDGED FOR THEIR SINS because of My Son's sacrifice, and they continue to love the world and the things of the flesh. Do not cling to the things of this world, for they can neither save nor deliver you from what is coming. Those of you who walk with Me will receive My strength and My power to prevail on the earth in the face of what will seem like utter madness.

Many of you have been concerned with the storing of food or weapons, but I tell you now neither food nor weapons will be able to save you from this wrath. Store up My Word instead—hide it in your hearts for the dark days ahead, for you shall need its power then to survive.

Rejoice! Rejoice, My children, for your time on the earth is short, and soon you will arrive home and be free!

1 Timothy 3:1: This know also, that in the last days perilous times shall come.

1 Samuel 12:21: And turn ye not aside: for then should ye go after vain things, which cannot profit nor deliver; for they are vain.

Deut. 11:18: Therefore shall ye lay up these my words in your heart and in your soul, and bind them for a sign upon your hand, that they may be as frontlets between your eyes.

Eph. 5:2: And walk in love, as Christ also hath loved us, and hath given himself for us an offering and a sacrifice to God for a sweet smelling savour.

2 John 1:6: And this is love, that we walk after his commandments. This is the commandment, That, as ye have heard from the beginning, ye should walk in it.

1 Peter 3:15: But sanctify the Lord God in your hearts: and be ready always to give an answer to every man that asketh you a reason of the hope that is in you with meekness and fear:

1/15/11

A GREAT SAVING, HEALING, DELIVERING AND PSALMS MINISTRY IS COMING TO THIS NATION

A great saving, healing, delivering, and psalms ministry is coming to this nation (America). No longer will My sheep scatter and run from a tainted church, for I shall birth ministries this year in America and raise up prophets who speak My Word with boldness and without fear. I shall call forth ministers of My gospel that are true to My commands and who obey only Me— those who will not compromise or water down My message.

Gone will be the days of wicked shepherds leading My precious sheep astray. You will know My true shepherds by the fire in their voices, the fire in their message. You shall know them by their works, by the fruit that comes forth from these ministries. You will know it is I who work through them by the things they do. You will know they are Mine beyond any shadow of a doubt, for they will speak only that which agrees with My Holy Word.

Great miracles, signs and wonders are about to break out in this nation like never before. Healings My people have waited decades for will suddenly manifest. Limbs will be grown where none were before. Blind eyes not only opened, but eyes borne into sockets that were previously empty, in front of large crowds of people.

Know when you see these, that you are seeing My hands at work. Know that a mighty God is in your midst and show Me reverence, for I will surely punish those who do not. Flocks of people—those who never sought Me before—will suddenly begin to inquire about the God they never understood. Be ready, My people, be ready with answers from My Word for these lost sheep when they run to you. Be ready to give an answer from My Word, to tell them of My glory, of My mighty power to save, deliver, and set free.

The days of the yawning church are coming to an end, and My true ministers will rise like flames of fire across this dry land. They will speak forth My Word; and miracles—mighty miracles—will follow wherever My true gospel is preached. Unbelievers will convert by the thousands in this time. The harvest is great, My people, but truly the laborers have been few who truly loved the sheep, who truly fed My sheep, who truly led My sheep. But no more, for I am coming back soon, and I desire to find a church alive with My holy presence, alive with My power. A church this lost, hurting, and broken world runs to, instead of away from.

Watch this year as I raise up a new and prophetic generation of ministers, the likes of which you have never seen before. They are peculiar and they are Mine. They shall be My true voice to My people, for those who do not truly speak My words I shall cut off.

Hebrews 2:3-4: How shall we escape, if we neglect so great salvation; which at the first began to be spoken by the Lord, and was confirmed unto us by them that heard him; God also bearing them witness, both with signs and wonders, and with divers miracles, and gifts of the Holy Ghost, according to his own will?

Matt. 7:20: Wherefore by their fruits ye shall know them.

Mark 16:17: And these signs shall follow them that believe; In my name shall they cast out devils; they shall speak with new tongues.

Psalm 104:4: Who maketh his angels spirits; his ministers a flaming fire.

Luke 10:2: Therefore said he unto them, The harvest truly is great, but the labourers are few: pray ye therefore the Lord of the harvest, that he would send forth labourers into his harvest.

1 Peter 3:15: But sanctify the Lord God in your hearts: and be ready always to give an answer to every man that asketh you a reason of the hope that is in you with meekness and fear.

Titus 2:14: Who gave himself for us, that he might redeem us from all iniquity, and purify unto himself a peculiar people, zealous of good works.

1/17/11

A TIME OF MANY DANGERS

My people, you are coming into a time of many dangers. Dangers will lurk all around you, and many of them will be unseen to the human eye. For this reason I have been calling many of you to come into a place of more intimacy with Me. I desire to shield you under the protection of My mighty wings, but many of you have been too busy for Me.

"Later, Lord," you keep saying. What you do not know is that for many of you, later will never come, for calamity shall strike and you will be unprepared, so busy are you with the things of the world.

I speak this warning to you now: IF YOU DO NOT MAKE TIME FOR ME NOW, I WILL NOT BE ABLE TO PROTECT YOU FROM WHAT IS COMING. You are worried about many things, but I desire you to cast your cares on Me; let Me carry your burdens, My child. You need only be mindful of spending time with Me, of seeking My face; and all the other things you need will fall into place.

Do you not see? Do you not know? The time of the end has come and My bride is not prepared! MANY OF YOU HAVE NOT

YET LEARNED HOW TO SEEK MY FACE, HOW TO HEAR MY VOICE, AND YOU ARE NOT READY FOR WHAT IS ABOUT TO HAPPEN IN THE EARTH.

Disasters—great disasters of a magnitude you cannot even comprehend—are coming; and many of My people discern not the times in their spirits!

Delve deeper into My Word—deeper than ever before—and I shall reveal to you the treasures of knowledge I have hidden there for these last days. Come higher with Me—higher than ever before—and I will reveal to you the things you know not of!

Oh My children, I long to give you all the riches of My Kingdom in this time, but I cannot if you will not even make room for Me in your busy lives!

Come to Me! Call on My Name and cry out for more of Me, and I shall gladly answer and fill you with My Spirit. Do not wait any longer. The time of the end is near!

Psalm 91:4: He shall cover thee with his feathers, and under his wings shalt thou trust: his truth shall be thy shield and buckler.

1 Peter 5:7: Casting all your care upon him; for he careth for you.

Isaiah 45:3: And I will give thee the treasures of darkness, and hidden riches of secret places, that thou mayest know that I, the LORD, which call thee by thy name, am the God of Israel.

1/20/11

INCREASE IN WORDS RELEASED

There will be an increase in My words released through My prophets in days to come. I desire for My people to repent while there is yet time. Some of you I will send into dark places— strange places you have not known—to deliver these words and to do My will there. Some of you I will call into prayer. Many of you I will call to come aside with Me.

It is time for My people to simplify their lives. Pare down, My people, pare down the excesses, the unnecessary, the superficial elements of your life, for in times to come this will be a help to you.

Catastrophe is about to strike the nation of America in a way all nations shall be affected, and My people are not prepared. I have shown great love to this nation, but she has turned her back on Me, and her ways are no longer My ways.

My people have ignored My words and turned away from My precepts and walked in their own ways. Their hearts have grown farther from Me, and their lives have become entwined in the world in which they live. In times to come, this shall not be so, for if they neglect to draw near to Me, they shall perish from the earth.

My people, do you not know? Do you not yet understand that you cannot survive what is coming without Me? Do you not know I long for the sound of your voice calling out for Me? I long for our intimate times together, for you to draw near to Me and seek My face. I desire that you would seek My heart in the matters of your life and not follow your own.

Many of you have filled your time with worldly pleasures, with distractions, and the entertainments of the time you live in; and you have forgotten Me. You do not realize the true price of these distractions.

Psalm 9:17: The wicked shall be turned into hell, and all the nations that forget God. For the needy shall not always be forgotten: the expectation of the poor shall not perish forever.

Daniel 9:5-6: We have sinned, and have committed iniquity, and have done wickedly, and have rebelled, even by departing from thy precepts and from thy judgments: Neither have we hearkened unto thy servants the prophets, which spake in thy name to our kings, our princes, and our fathers, and to all the people of the land.

Isaiah 29:13: Wherefore the Lord said, Forasmuch as this people draw near me with their mouth, and with their lips do honour me, but have removed their heart far from me, and their fear toward me is taught by the precept of men.

Psalm 73:28: But it is good for me to draw near to God: I have put my trust in the Lord GOD, that I may declare all thy works.

Titus 2:12: Teaching us that, denying ungodliness and worldly lusts, we should live soberly, righteously, and godly, in this present world.

James 4:8: Draw nigh to God, and he will draw nigh to you. Cleanse your hands, ye sinners; and purify your hearts, ye double minded.

1/28/11

AS YOU HAVE SOWN YOU WILL REAP

As you have sown, so shall you now reap, My children. Be careful that the words you speak and the ways in which you have dealt with others is fair and reputable, for I shall <u>now</u> begin repaying all that you have done, both good and bad. If you have done evil, repent. If you have done well, then I shall reward you with good.

For too long have My children frolicked in the ways of this world, instead of keeping their eyes on Me. Many of you care more for prospering your own reputation than you do Mine; and you shall be found as clouds with no rain for your efforts, for I cannot bless what is not of Me.

For those of you who have turned from Me to the world, know that your Day of Judgment is at hand, and all you have done is soon to come back upon your own heads. *Your hands are not clean, and your hearts have not been purified in the fires of My refining, for you chose not to stay where I placed you but ran after your own ways.*

WOE TO YOU who plan your own footsteps and follow your own plans in days to come, for you shall not know where to run as My judgment begins to fall in your lives.

WOE TO YOU who call upon and trust in other gods, for they can neither save nor deliver you from what is coming.

WOE TO YOU, inhabitants of earth, for Satan has come down to you with great wrath and the end is near.

WOE TO YOU who prophesy lies and lead My children astray, for you yourselves shall also be deceived. As you have sown, so shall you reap. Thus saith the Lord of Hosts.

This year shall be a time of reaping what has been sown both in the natural and the spiritual. If you have sown strife, you shall now reap the same. If you have sown deception, you shall reap it. But if you have sown love and obedience, you shall now reap the rewards of My Kingdom.

Be careful that you do not deceive yourselves, My children, for many of you think you stand when you are deceived. Bring your hearts before Me as an offering, and I will cleanse them with My refining fire, for I shall burn everything out that is not of Me. For you look at others as through a magnifying glass but examine yourselves by other standards. An unjust weight is an abomination in My sight. Check your hearts, My children! Check your hearts that you may be found fit for My use in Kingdom work, for many of you think you are working for Me, but you carry out the work of the enemy of your souls!

Remove from your lives what is not of Me and all that is not pure and holy like Me. Cleanse your hands that I may use them for Kingdom work! Do not come before Me any longer with the sins of the world staining your hands, but walk before Me clean, pure, and holy.

Why look you to your own things? Turn your eyes to your brother in need. Turn your heart to the lost and broken in the world of sin in which you live.

Gal. 6:7: Be not deceived; God is not mocked: for whatsoever a man soweth, that shall he also reap.

Gal 6:8: For he that soweth to his flesh shall of the flesh reap corruption; but he that soweth to the Spirit shall of the Spirit reap life everlasting.

Job 4:8: Even as I have seen, they that plow iniquity, and sow wickedness, reap the same.

Hosea 10:12: Sow to yourselves in righteousness, reap in mercy; break up your fallow ground: for it is time to seek the LORD, till he come and rain righteousness upon you.

2 Cor. 9:6: But this I say, He which soweth sparingly shall reap also sparingly; and he which soweth bountifully shall reap also bountifully.

1 Cor. 10:12: Wherefore let him that thinketh he standeth take heed lest he fall.

Rev. 12:12: Therefore rejoice, ye heavens, and ye that dwell in them. Woe to the inhabiters of the earth and of the seal for the devil is come down unto you, having great wrath, because he knoweth that he hath but a short time.

Mal. 3:2-3: But who may abide the day of his coming? and who shall stand when he appeareth? for he is like a refiner's fire, and like fullers' soap: And he shall sit as a refiner and purifier of silver: and he shall purify the sons of Levi, and purge them as gold and silver, that they may offer unto the LORD an offering in righteousness.

James 4:8: Draw nigh to God, and he will draw nigh to you. Cleanse your hands, ye sinners; and purify your hearts, ye double minded.

2/16/11

SUBMIT TO ME

My children, you pray to Me for more revelation, and yet you resist when you are tried. YOU RESIST ME WHEN I AM WALKING YOU INTO THE VERY EVENTS THAT WILL BRING ABOUT THE REVELATIONS YOU ASKED ME FOR. Submit. Submit to My guidance and My refining, for this will bring about great and mighty changes in your lives that you have asked Me for.

Many of you are about to face big changes in your life. These changes will be unexpected, and you will have the opportunity to get into fear or to trust Me. Trust Me, and I will bring you through what is happening. If you choose to fear and not believe, from where will your help come? For I said to Fear Not.

The changes that are coming are necessary so I may position you for what is coming next. Do not resist My change in your lives, for it is necessary to your wellbeing, and only I know what the next step in your plan is. Many of you have suffered great attacks from the enemy on your homes, your families, your bodies. These attacks will increase in days to come as he knows his time is running out, and he is desperate for souls for his kingdom. Take care yours does not become one of the souls he is about to snatch.

Job 23:10: But he knoweth the way that I take: when he hath tried me, I shall come forth as gold.

Daniel 12:10: Many shall be purified, and made white, and tried; but the wicked shall do wickedly: and none of the wicked shall understand; but the wise shall understand.

Zech. 13:9: And I will bring the third part through the fire, and will refine them as silver is refined, and will try them as gold is tried: they shall call on my name, and I will hear them: I will say, It is my people: and they shall say, The LORD is my God.

3/01/11

MY CHOSEN ONES

I am about to exalt some of those I have been preparing to carry My glory in hidden places. Soon you will all know who My chosen ones are as I bring them to the forefront and raise up large ministries through them.

Some of you also had I chosen to be among these, but you have refused to walk in My ways and speak My truths; and as I exalt your brothers and sisters who did obey Me, you shall also know who you are that I cannot exalt because you would not obey Me.

Many of you know the path to which you have been called, and you have refused to set your feet to My paths. You fear loss, you fear reproach, you fear even fear itself, but did I not say "Fear not?" Have I not been faithful to you, oh ye of little faith? Have I not carried you in hard times and taught you in good times?

Am I or am I not your Mighty God?

I shall speak to you soon, chosen ones, and tell you what you must do for Me in order that I may exalt you to a higher place, that you may carry My Name and reflect My glory. I shall speak to you in the night seasons. Be ready, oh bride and listen, for your Bridegroom cometh.

Joshua 24:22: And Joshua said unto the people, Ye are witnesses against yourselves that ye have chosen you the LORD, to serve him. And they said, We are witnesses.

Psalm 105:43: And he brought forth his people with joy, and his chosen with gladness.

Joel 2:16: Gather the people, sanctify the congregation, assemble the elders, gather the children, and those that suck the breasts: let the bridegroom go forth of his chamber, and the bride out of her closet.

Matthew 23:12: And whosoever shall exalt himself shall be abased; and he that shall humble himself shall be exalted.

1 Peter 5:6: Humble yourselves therefore under the mighty hand of God, that he may exalt you in due time.

Psalm 118:6: The LORD is on my side; I will not fear: what can man do unto me?

Isaiah 41:10: Fear thou not; for I am with thee: be not dismayed; for I am thy God: I will strengthen thee; yea, I will help thee; yea, I will uphold thee with the right hand of my righteousness.

3/15/11

THIS IS THE CALM BEFORE THE STORM

This is the calm before the storm. Soon a storm will rage in the U.S. as it has raged in Japan, inciting fear and panic among its people.

My children have no need to fear, for they shall truly be found in Me, but woe to those who have refused Me! Woe to those whose hearts have been given to other gods, for truly this world shall become a terror to them.

Run, My people! Run under My wings when you see the storm coming, for I shall protect you and keep you safe! I shall supply all your need as you go about in the earth serving Me and witnessing of Me.

Be found in Me! Purify your hearts before Me and yield yourselves to My service like never before, for the door soon shuts on the Marriage Feast of the Lamb, and woe to those found outside the door.

Psalm 46:1: God is our refuge and strength, a very present help in trouble.

Psalm 59:16: But I will sing of thy power; yea, I will sing aloud of thy mercy in the morning: for thou hast been my defense and refuge in the day of my trouble.

Psalm 91:2: I will say of the Lord, He is my refuge and my fortress: my God; in him will I trust.

Isaiah 41:10: Fear thou not; for I am with thee: be not dismayed; for I am thy God: I will strengthen thee; yea, I will help thee; yea, I will uphold thee with the right hand of my righteousness.

Psalm 17:8: Keep me as the apple of the eye, hide me under the shadow of thy wings,

Psalm 57:1: Be merciful unto me, O God, be merciful unto me: for my soul trusteth in thee: yea, in the shadow of thy wings will I make my refuge, until these calamities be overpast.

Luke 13:25: When once the master of the house is risen up, and hath shut to the door, and ye begin to stand without, and to knock at the door, saying, Lord, Lord, open unto us; and he shall answer and say unto you, I know you not whence ye are.

Rev. 19:9: And he saith unto me, Write, Blessed are they which are called unto the marriage supper of the Lamb. And he saith unto me, These are the true sayings of God.

3/17/11

VIOLENT UPHEAVALS COMING

Not long ago, I was praying about the intense feeling I have experienced since New Years 2011 that a devastating earthquake is going to happen soon in America. Instead of talking to me about the coming earthquake I was feeling, the Lord showed me a vision of earthquakes in the lives of believers. I didn't understand the meaning of the vision and prayed that He would reveal what it meant.

Last night as I was praying again, He showed me more. *I saw violent upheavals that will soon be coming into the lives of believers. The shaking will be both sudden and unexpected.*

He is trying to get you somewhere, and what doesn't make it through the shaking are things and people that need to be removed for His plan for your life to move forward. *I saw a violent shaking that caused everything to fly into chaos, and when the pieces landed, not all of them were there, but the ones that were, were in perfect position, and the Lord smiled upon this.*

This shaking will be coming to the strongest believers, not baby Christians. The Lord said He is going to be shaking some of you soon and that He has a purpose in it and that He wants you to remain calm when it happens and trust Him.

The Lord is saying: *Lean on Me, and learn to have My peace in your spirit in the midst of chaos, for soon you will need this.*

Do not fear.

3/25/11

OBEY ME NOW

Perilous times are upon you in the earth. Many are the schemes of those behind the scenes who have the power to divide and conquer. Many are the ways of their plans to defeat the will of the people to do what is right, to bring down those who bear My Name in the earth.

Yet it is not their faces nor plans you need fear, My children, but the hand of your God if you do not obey Me. For My plans shall go forth and be carried out in the earth at this time, and woe to those who refuse to walk in My ways and do My will in these times, for they shall face the enemy without My wisdom or power to guide them in what they should do.

Woe to those who languish in earthly pleasure and do not know the lateness of the hour at hand, for quickly shall I come, and they shall be left behind and face a fate far worse than mere death.

Great will be the reward of those who will follow Me and My will to the ends of the earth in these last days. Great and mighty will be the power they walk in and the glory they behold! THEY SHALL WITNESS SIGNS AND WONDERS SUCH AS NOTHING THIS WORLD HAS EVER WITNESSED BEFORE, and great shall be their reward in Heaven for enduring.

I will speak in time soon coming to many of you of what I would have you to do for My Name's sake. Be quick to obey, My children, for the time draws near for the Bridegroom's return.

Do not linger in seeking pleasure or chasing the things of this world, for you shall soon be leaving them behind. Trust Me to supply your needs. For did I not promise in My Word that I would do this for those who would walk in My ways?

Do not be deceived, My children, into thinking the hour is not as late as it is, for that is what the enemy desires for you to believe; and if you linger at the pleasures of the world or refuse My commands, you will truly know regret. For the time is past for lingering and refusing to obey. I AM real, I AM alive, and I AM watching to see if you will obey. If you will not obey Me and obey quickly, I shall pass your task to another.

At this point, the Lord said there will be some who are hearing this word and are still refusing to obey Him. To you, He says: *Obey Me now or face My judgment on your life.*

Then you will cry, "Father! Where is my reward?" But I say to you that I passed that also to one more willing to sacrifice comfort, more willing to hear Me and obey, for you were not willing.

Make haste, My children. It is time to return from playing now and address the seriousness of the hour. You have heard My words; now obey Me that you may escape the worst of what is soon to come upon the earth.

Luke 12:47: And that servant, which knew his lord's will, and prepared not himself, neither did according to his will, shall be beaten with many stripes.

2 Tim. 3:1: This know also, that in the last days perilous times shall come.

Matt. 7:21: Not every one that saith unto me, Lord, Lord, shall enter into the kingdom of heaven; but he that doeth the will of my Father which is in heaven.

Isaiah 30:1: Woe to the rebellious children, saith the LORD, that take counsel, but not of me; and that cover with a covering, but not of my spirit, that they may add sin to sin.

1 Sam. 15:22-29: And Samuel said, Hath the LORD as great delight in burnt offerings and sacrifices, as in obeying the voice of the LORD? Behold, to obey is better than sacrifice, and to hearken than the fat of rams.

23. For rebellion is as the sin of witchcraft, and stubbornness is as iniquity and idolatry. Because thou hast rejected the Word of the LORD, he hath also rejected thee from being king.

24. And Saul said unto Samuel, I have sinned: for I have transgressed the commandment of the LORD, and thy words: because I feared the people, and obeyed their voice.

25. Now therefore, I pray thee, pardon my sin, and turn again with me, that I may worship the LORD.

26. And Samuel said unto Saul, I will not return with thee: for thou hast rejected the Word of the LORD, and the LORD hath rejected thee from being king over Israel.

27. And as Samuel turned about to go away, he laid hold upon the skirt of his mantle, and it rent.

28. And Samuel said unto him, The LORD hath rent the kingdom of Israel from thee this day, and hath given it to a neighbour of thine, that is better than thou.

29. And also the Strength of Israel will not lie nor repent: for he is not a man that he should repent.

3/31/11

AMERICA WILL SUFFER MANY WOUNDS

My people, you have come to a crossroads. You will no longer live in a world where you can sit on a fence about your belief in Me. You must choose you this day whom you will serve and be sure of it. Be sure of Me, for very soon your belief in Me will become a public thing. You will be ridiculed, mocked, even beaten for your beliefs. Yes, even in America, the land once so proud to bear My Name, that no longer resembles Me. I no longer call it My own, for it has no desire to serve Me. Once so blessed, so full of abundance, it will soon no longer be.

For when you reject Me, you also reject the blessings I bring. You cannot reject one and not the other. We are one. America has chosen her ways over Mine; she will now reap the consequences of her choices.

My children, very difficult times lie just ahead for you who are called by My Name. Those who are not truly Mine will quickly defect when choices must be made that carry a high price. When it is no longer convenient for them to say they are Mine, they will no longer be. It is that simple.

Woe unto those who choose the way of unrighteousness, for they shall dwell in darkness!

For you who are My own, prepare your hearts to be steadfast in Me, for that is the only way you shall endure what is just ahead for you all. I will give you strength and wisdom for what you must face.

Many of you in the last several years on earth have endured very trying times. This was My way of strengthening you, and you shall soon see that it was necessary to take you that way when you see what is ahead.

Pray. Pray often for those you love, and pray for strength to endure what is coming to this nation, for it will be like nothing you have seen before. America in its pride has wounded many other countries, and now she herself will suffer many wounds.

Draw near to Me. Let me hide you under My wings from the worst of what is to come. Let Me sing songs of deliverance over you as I protect you with My strong hand from all I must do to judge this sinful nation.

4/07/11

A YEAR OF MUCH CHANGE

This is the time of your preparation. As these days unfold, I will be guiding you into what preparations you personally need to make for what is coming to the earth. It is different for each of My children, so do not think you can prepare the same way as your brothers and sisters. Only I know the extent of each peril and where each event will take place. Only I know which of you need to prepare and which do not. Listen only to My voice, and I will guide you in what you should do to get ready.

I have stationed many of you near areas where perils will come. Because they happen near you and you are affected, do not think My hand of protection was not upon you, for if I remove My hand, you would surely perish. You and all your household.

Some of what you see in coming days and months will be My righteous judgments; some are only warnings to those who need to repent. Both are necessary. My plan which was formed before the foundations of the world as you know it, is all about to play out before your eyes. Keep your eyes fastened on Me, My children, and your mind will be at peace. If you take your eyes off Me and look at what is happening around you, the enemy will surely ensnare you to fear for your lives, when there is no need. Your days and your times are all in My mighty hands, so there is no need for you to fear.

At the end of this year, many of your lives will be forever changed. These changes shall come in various ways. Did I not say this would be a year of much change? It will be a year of much intensity as well. Take heed lest the enemy use this emotional intensity to wear you down and to discourage you, for this year shall indeed bring many changes you know not of.

Expect the unexpected, My children, for this year you shall see it. My judgments have begun, and they have begun in My own house, in My own people. You will see in days to come results of these judgments. I will no longer allow corruption to remain hidden from view while I plead with My people to repent. Those who have been warned to repent and did not turn from their sins will now face My judgment on their lives. It will not be pretty to see. Pray for your brothers and sisters, My children, for they shall need every prayer you can muster, as I bring gross corruption and perversion to the forefront of the headlines and expose what they would not repent of and turn away from. There is no other way.

Remember to restore your brothers and sisters. Do not hide from them, but reach out to them in love and restore one another in love lest you yourself be next to fall.

Many unknowns shall rise to stardom in this time. They are My chosen ones, those I have been preparing quietly for many years now. Many times have they come before Me and asked Me "When, Lord? When will be the fulfillment of all you have promised me?" I say to you now, My children, your time to rise is now. You are called and you are chosen, and I have made known to you who you are. Now obey Me in all I say to do, and I shall exalt you into all I have promised you. Not one promise shall be left unfulfilled if you obey all I say.

Worship Me. Worship Me now for all I have coming to you. For your future is bright and beautiful and full of My glory, and you shall surely delight in all I have brought you into when you begin to see the promised land.

Take heed, My children. Take heed you do not stumble at this time, for the enemy seeks to destroy you, and he has increased his attacks on My people in these end times. You must be more vigilant that ever before. You must walk worthy of the calling I have placed on your life. You must not give in to temptation or look back at what you have left behind, for there is little time left now. Finish the race for Me; finish the race in faithfulness and in truth. Do all I have called you to do for My Name's sake.

Many will be the obstacles the enemy shall place in your way in an attempt to stop you from completing what you have been chosen to do. Overcome him! Overcome. I have given you all you need to overcome every plan, every obstacle, every attack from the enemy. If you need more wisdom, you need only ask Me and I will give it to you. But do not stop fighting the enemy, My children, for he seeks to destroy you. He seeks to destroy all that is of Me.

You will need all your strength in this final hour. Gird your loins well—feast on My Word and be ready when he attacks you. Be ready, for he is coming to you.

He will send attacks against you—both large and small—to defeat you, to tire you out, to wear you down, to discourage you. Whenever you feel these things, know it is the enemy and resist him, My children. Be watchful. Watch and pray. Do not sleep in this final hour. Do not let your guard down and let your heart go out to play, for there is no time now for playing. My soldiers must stand ready for battle in this final hour.

Be ready.

Isaiah 26:3: Thou wilt keep him in perfect peace, whose mind is stayed on thee: because he trusteth in thee.

1 Peter 4:17: For the time is come that judgment must begin at the house of God: and if it first begin at us, what shall the end be of them that obey not the gospel of God?

Gal. 6:1: Brethren, if a man be overtaken in a fault, ye which are spiritual, restore such an one in the spirit of meekness; considering thyself, lest thou also be tempted.

Isaiah 1:19: If ye be willing and obedient, ye shall eat the good of the land.

Eph. 4:1: I therefore, the prisoner of the Lord, beseech you that ye walk worthy of the vocation wherewith ye are called,

Luke 9:62: And Jesus said unto him, No man, having put his hand to the plough, and looking back, is fit for the kingdom of God.

Heb. 12:1-2: Wherefore seeing we also are compassed about with so great a cloud of witnesses, let us lay aside every weight, and the sin which doth so easily beset us, and let us run with patience the race that is set before us, Looking unto Jesus the author and finisher of our faith; who for the joy that was set before him endured the cross, despising the shame, and is set down at the right hand of the throne of God.

Romans 12:21: Be not overcome of evil, but overcome evil with good.

James 1:5: If any of you lack wisdom, let him ask of God, that giveth to all men liberally, and upbraideth not; and it shall be given him.

Luke 12:35-36: Let your loins be girded about, and your lights burning; And ye yourselves like unto men that wait for their lord, when he will return from the wedding; that when he cometh and knocketh, they may open unto him immediately.

1 Peter 1:13: Wherefore gird up the loins of your mind, be sober, and hope to the end for the grace that is to be brought unto you at the revelation of Jesus Christ;

John 10:10: The thief cometh not, but for to steal, and to kill, and to destroy: I am come that they might have life, and that they might have it more abundantly.

1 Peter 5:8: Be sober, be vigilant; because your adversary the devil, as a roaring lion, walketh about, seeking whom he may devour.

Mark 13:33: Take ye heed, watch and pray: for ye know not when the time is.

4/14/11

THE TIME OF MY GREAT WARRIORS

I was shown a vision of a stormy sea—very large black waves were crashing down and wrapping around, crashing against each other. All around the waves I could see only darkness. It looked like the darkest of stormy nights.

The word "turmoil" came to my mind. In the midst of the turmoil of all the crashing waves, a small light appeared over the horizon—like an approaching ship or a distant lighthouse. But very quickly the waves swallowed up the light and it was gone. Then I saw a frozen landscape, as if in the dead of winter.

I have no idea what the frozen landscape meant. The following morning, the Lord began to speak.

Times are about to become very difficult in the world, My children. There is no time for playing games. All your time must be focused on preparation for what is to come and on walking in your calling. Remove now the excesses from your lives, as I have been speaking to your hearts to do. Lighten the load you carry, for you cannot carry as heavy a load on an uphill run, and that is what is coming for you. Big changes loom on the horizon behind the scenes that will affect your everyday lives.

Be careful to show kindness to each other, to walk in My love towards one another, as this will shield you from many of the attacks of the enemy and help you to remain focused.

I will be moving in many of your lives in coming months, orchestrating the changes I desire, to make you more fit for kingdom use and to strategically position you for the things I have called you to do. Do not fight against My changes, for they are necessary, and unless you submit to Me in them, you cannot be of full benefit to My Kingdom.

Turmoil is coming to many governments in the next two months. This is My hand at work, though it will not seem so to many. Many of My own people do not understand the many avenues I work through. All that is of peace is not of Me, and all that is of war is not either. Nothing happens that I do not allow, and the enemy's plans come as no surprise to Me, for I see all and know all.

My Word holds the key to understanding all things. My Word is My most precious gift to you, My children—My Word, My Son. If you walk by My Word, you walk in wisdom, and the world has no effect on you.

Those who ignore the power in My Word will fall quickly in times coming, for they will not know how to stand against the enemy's onslaught on My people. Be diligent therefore in studying My Word, that you may live and not die. Those who have ears to hear, hear and obey.

I have sent many to warn of what is coming, but many still walk in darkness. Many walk in folly, not believing. They shall be taken quickly, unawares, for they did not believe My Word. All you need to survive you have in My Word. In it is wisdom and guidance. In it are hidden treasures of great price that you know not of.

Those who obey Me shall survive what is coming. Yeah, not only survive, but prosper in it, for this will be the time of My great warriors. This will be the time of the lifting up, of the showing forth of those I have been preparing behind closed doors. This is your time, My chosen ones. Now is your time to shine before I finally bring you home to Me!

How I long for the day when you all enter into My rest and are all here with Me! I love you with an everlasting love without measure. I long to have you near Me, to hear your voice whisper My Name, to know you trust fully in Me in all things. Draw near to Me and seek Me in these dark times, and you shall find Me and we shall be as one. I will hold you close to Me. I will cover you with My feathers, and as you see displays of My mighty power, you will not feel afraid at all, for I shall protect you as a good shepherd protects the flock, for you are Mine and I love you with a jealous love!

What is soon coming is the dark night of the soul for some—those who are not ready—a time of revealing for those who are. This will be My time to reveal to the world who you truly are in Me. MANY WILL STAND IN AWE OF THE GIFTS I HAVE PLACED IN YOU AND OF MY MIGHTY POWER WORKING THROUGH YOU. Be sure you give Me the glory, My children. Woe to those who try to take My glory for themselves, for destruction comes quickly to them!

Now is a time of much prayer. Pray that you may walk worthy through the turmoil that is coming. Pray that you will not be found wanting in any way. Pray that you will be ready to step into all I have called you to do for My Name's sake. Pray that you do not stumble in the way, for the battle is quickly approaching. Pray for your brothers and sisters. Pray for each other to be strengthened and made ready in every possible way.

In days to come I will begin to remove obstacles from your path, that you may serve Me more fully and efficiently. Watch for these things to happen, and inquire of Me about what changes I would have you to make at that time, for when I do this, I have a purpose for what was freed up.

Some of you will hear from Me soon, to move or to reposition yourselves for My purposes. Know that I will bring you the means and ways to do so when the time comes; and do not fear, for there is always provision on the path to which I have called you, and to believe otherwise is to believe a lie from the enemy. If you have no provision, check that the path you are on is truly the way I have called you to go, for many times My children take a wrong turn and think I do not provide, but this is never the case. I am a loving and faithful provider.

Hard times are coming, My children. Times like nothing you have ever encountered before, but I have already spoken provision for you into existence. Look for it, for it shall surely appear.

Prepare well. Prepare to run the race set before you for My glory!

John 1:14: And the Word was made flesh, and dwelt among us, (and we beheld his glory, the glory as of the only begotten of the Father,) full of grace and truth.

Matthew 13:9: Who hath ears to hear, let him hear.

Isaiah 45:3: And I will give thee the treasures of darkness, and hidden riches of secret places, that thou mayest know that I, the LORD, which call thee by thy name, am the God of Israel.

Jeremiah 6:10: To whom shall I speak, and give warning, that they may hear? behold, their ear is uncircumcised, and they cannot hearken: behold, the word of the LORD is unto them a reproach; they have no delight in it.

Ezekiel 33:4: Then whosoever heareth the sound of the trumpet, and taketh not warning; if the sword come, and take him away, his blood shall be upon his own head.

Psalm 91:4: He shall cover thee with his feathers, and under his wings shalt thou trust: his truth shall be thy shield and buckler.

Luke 22:32: But I have prayed for thee, that thy faith fail not: and when thou art converted, strengthen thy brethren.

Deut. 4:24: For the LORD thy God is a consuming fire, even a jealous God.

Isaiah 45:2: I will go before thee, and make the crooked places straight: I will break in pieces the gates of brass, and cut in sunder the bars of iron.

Acts 12:21-23: And upon a set day Herod, arrayed in royal apparel, sat upon his throne, and made an oration unto them. And the people gave a shout, saying, It is the voice of a god, and not of a man. And immediately the angel of the Lord smote him, because he gave not God the glory: and he was eaten of worms, and gave up the ghost.

4/15/11

YOU HAVE HEARD THE WARNING SOUND

The doctrines of men have deceived you into lethargy, My people! Awake! Awake and rise up to your posts, for many of you shall perish in what is coming soon if you do not.

You have believed the lies of the enemy that there is still more time, that no battle approaches, that the end is nowhere near here; but you have been deceived. You have believed these things that you may not fear what is ahead, that you might remain in the world following your own desires; but I say to you now the world shall become a snare to you as the hunter approaches.

At this point, I saw a brief vision of a small animal caught in the steel jaws of a trap, wildly trying to free itself, and the large black form of a hunter, who I knew was very evil, was approaching it.

Repent! Repent of your lethargy and unwillingness to believe My words now—before it is too late for you; for many of you shall be taken in what is soon to come, and you know it not.

So many of you are not ready. Would you go to war with no preparations beforehand? Would you walk into battle with no guide? And yet you walk blindly forward to your own destruction because you refuse to believe My words.

Prepare ye well, My people. Study My Word that you may fight your enemy valiantly in the battle soon coming! Do not be found wanting in My eyes, for the consequences are grave indeed.

You have heard the warning sound.

Repent and return to your post before it is too late.

Get ready, for the battle is quickly approaching when you shall be made to fight. Darkness is coming. Days of great darkness lay ahead for My people everywhere.

Those without My Word shining brightly in their hearts shall not be able to endure this great onslaught of the enemy, for it shall come from many directions at once and be very fierce indeed, for he knows his time is short now.

Many of My people are now preparing behind the scenes, but many are not even paying heed to the many warnings I have sent them. Soon the battle will be upon you, and there will be no more time to prepare. IT WILL BE TOO LATE THEN FOR THOSE WHO HAVE IGNORED MY WORDS, AND MANY SHALL PERISH BECAUSE OF IT. Many will enter into eternal darkness, for they loved not the light of My glorious Word.

I have given you power over every device of the wicked one, but that power is hidden in My Word. It is not your physical bodies nor in your physical preparations. The power you will need to fight this battle can only be found in My Word.

Matthew 15:9: But in vain they do worship me, teaching for doctrines the commandments of men.

John 3:19: And this is the condemnation, that light is come into the world, and men loved darkness rather than light, because their deeds were evil.

Luke 10:19: Behold, I give unto you power to tread on serpents and scorpions, and over all the power of the enemy: and nothing shall by any means hurt you.

Isaiah 45:3: And I will give thee the treasures of darkness, and hidden riches of secret places, that thou mayest know that I, the LORD, which call thee by thy name, am the God of Israel.

Zechariah 4:6: Then he answered and spake unto me, saying, This is the Word of the LORD unto Zerubbabel, saying, Not by might, nor by power, but by my spirit, saith the LORD of hosts.

4/17/11

YOUR TIME HAS COME

I was praying and asking the Lord about a shift in the Spirit I felt when I arose from sleep yesterday. I felt something had changed, but wasn't sure what it was or how it would affect us all.

There has indeed been a move of My Spirit during your sleep time. You will now notice time passing for you more quickly as I begin to bring all I have promised My chosen ones to pass now.

Ministries shall spring up quickly now as the wind of My favor blows and provision flows. Rejoice, My children, for now is truly your time to shine—shine for Me! Shine bright! Your light and My light will shine ever brighter now as the days begin to grow darker. Time is passing more quickly now—do you feel it, My children? Soon I will bring you home to be with Me here, but first you must do what I have called you to do. You know the plan I have given you. Put it into place and begin. Begin now. Work while it is still day, for time is short—short, indeed.

My winds of change are blowing now, and soon, very soon, things will not look the same. Many of you will not know where to turn as these changes begin because you have not heeded My words to you.

Those of you who have listened and obeyed shall fare well, for I shall now position you very quickly to do all that I have promised you I would do.

Take heart, My children. I know this last journey was a long one for you. I know many of your hearts fainted within you as you faced challenge after challenge, but I say to you now: Truly your time has come now.

You who have stood in faith on My Word, you who have stood against all odds on the promises I have given you for your lives—I shall now reward you greatly!

John 9:4: I must work the works of him that sent me, while it is day: the night cometh, when no man can work.

Lam. 5:17: For this our heart is faint; for these things our eyes are dim.

4/18/11

DECLARE UNTO ME NOW

It is a time to declare. Declare that which I have given you. Declare that which I have spoken to you, I will bring to pass. Declare it, for now it shall surely be done in the lives of all My children who have remained on the narrow path.

Declare unto Me now in faith those things I have promised, that you have been standing in faith for. Declare also that the enemy may not take them from you, that they are yours, for you shall surely walk in them now.

No longer shall those I have prepared remain in the shadows, for the brightness of My glory shining through them can no longer be hidden. This is the time of My chosen ones, and I shall now remove the veil from the eyes of those around you, My children, and they shall begin to see who you really are—who you were created to be, who you are in Me.

Get ready. Get ready to shine and prepare yourselves for all that that shall entail. Get ready to organize and administrate all that I am placing in your hands and in your power.

Walk in wisdom and manage it wisely. Walk before Me in purity of heart and mind. Walk before Me in diligence. Walk before Me in steadfastness, and do not waver from the path to which I have called you or the tasks which I have given you, for there is no time for stalling now.

Events will now begin transpiring in your life to bring about the changes that will place you in the ministries I have chosen for you. Stay in the flow of My Spirit. You will be in awe of how perfectly I am able to bring all to pass, just as I promised you I would; and joy shall overtake the weariness in your hearts and souls at this time.

Isaiah 42:9: Behold, the former things are come to pass, and new things do I declare: before they spring forth I tell you of them.

1 Cor. 4:2: Moreover it is required in stewards, that a man be found faithful.

Proverbs 4:23: Keep thy heart with all diligence; for out of it are the issues of life.

Phil. 4:8: Finally, brethren, whatsoever things are true, whatsoever things are honest, whatsoever things are just, whatsoever things are pure, whatsoever things are lovely, whatsoever things are of good report; if there be any virtue, and if there be any praise, think on these things.

Isaiah 61:3: To appoint unto them that mourn in Zion, to give unto them beauty for ashes, the oil of joy for mourning, the garment of praise for the spirit of heaviness; that they might be called trees of righteousness, the planting of the LORD, that he might be glorified.

4/21/11

TROUBLE COMING

There is trouble coming into the world, My children. You see trouble around you now, but it will grow far, far worse than this as this New Age dawns. The troubles you see before you now are very minute compared to what is soon to come.

Prepare your houses! Prepare your bodies and minds for the onslaught of the enemy that is coming, My children. I desire that you would stand tall and strong for Me in this time, that your hearts would be filled with courage as you face what lies just ahead, but many of you refuse to believe anything is coming at all. Many of you believe you will never suffer in this world, and that is not true. Did My Son not suffer? Did I spare Him? No, and you are joint heirs—not only in His blessings, but in His sufferings also.

Catastrophic events will cover the world before My Son comes back, for all nations shall be tested and shall be judged according to My Holy Word. My own children shall lose loved ones in some of these catastrophic events. As I said in My Word, there shall be famines, earthquakes, pestilences (plagues).

Turmoil in many governments is coming soon, sooner than you think, and it will bring confusion to many. Governments will fight amongst themselves. Kingdom shall rise up against kingdom. Sorrows will encompass you round about, but My love will encompass you even more. For those who abide in Me, it shall be a time of revealing My glory in all the earth.

IT WILL BE A TIME OF MANY MIRACLES, MIRACLES SUCH AS THIS WORLD HAS NEVER SEEN BEFORE, EVEN IN THE TIME OF MY SON!

Those who carry My glory throughout the earth will be tested and tried in every possible way. The enemy of your souls will do everything he can to stop you, to hinder your work—to delay you who are called and chosen from stepping into your call. He will try to destroy you once you have. He will attack your family members, your friends, your ministries. He will turn friends against you.

All this and more is coming in this time of great sorrow. But those who know Me, those who abide in Me and My Word, shall know great joy in this time in spite of the sorrows surrounding them round about. They shall stand courageous, speak My Word boldly, and bring glory to My Name. They shall cause many souls to come into the Kingdom in this time.

For those who do not answer My call, be prepared to give account. Be prepared to give an account to Me for what you have done with this life I have given you.

Look up, My children, for your redemption draweth nigh, but many sorrows come ahead of it. Do not fear when these things begin to happen, for they must happen according to My Word before My Son returns to the earth.

Yes, My children, trouble comes into the world now, but My love will surround you. Prepare your houses, prepare your minds for what is coming, for trouble shall visit every house upon the earth in this time.

1 Peter 4:13: But rejoice, inasmuch as ye are partakers of Christ's sufferings; that, when his glory shall be revealed, ye may be glad also with exceeding joy.

2 Cor. 1:5: For as the sufferings of Christ abound in us, so our consolation also aboundeth by Christ.

1 Peter 4:16: Yet if any man as a Christian, let him not be ashamed; but let him glorify God on this behalf.

Romans 8:18: For I reckon that the sufferings of this present time are not worthy to be compared with the glory which shall be revealed in us.

1 Peter 3:14: But and if ye suffer for righteousness' sake, happy are ye: and be not afraid of their terror, neither be troubled;

Matt. 24:7: For nation shall rise against nation, and kingdom against kingdom: and there shall be famines, and pestilences, and earthquakes, in divers places.

Matt. 24:8: All these are the beginning of sorrows.

Mark 13:8: For nation shall rise against nation, and kingdom against kingdom: and there shall be famines, and pestilences, and earthquakes, in divers places.

Luke 21:11: And great earthquakes shall be in divers places, and famines, and pestilences; and fearful sights and great signs shall there be from heaven.

Luke 21:28: And when these things begin to come to pass, then look up, and lift up your heads; for your redemption draweth nigh.

Rev. 9:20: And the rest of the men which were not killed by these plagues yet repented not of the works of their hands, that they should not worship devils, and idols of gold, and silver, and brass, and stone, and of wood: which neither can see, nor hear, nor walk:

John 14:12: Verily, verily, I say unto you, He that believeth on me, the works that I do shall he do also; and greater works than these shall he do; because I go unto my Father.

Job 23:10: But he knoweth the way that I take: when he hath tried me, I shall come forth as gold.

4/22/11

SITUATIONS NOT AS THEY APPEAR

Children, people are not always what they seem to be. Situations in the world are not as they appear to be. This will grow more and more with each day now as you move towards the end of time. People are able to deceive you, and situations are made to look like something else to suit the purposes of men and of the enemy; so much so that even My elect may be deceived in this time. Be careful that you discern what is really going on around you by seeking My face often. Be careful that you take nothing at face value. You must be ever more vigilant as time passes by, for many will seek to deceive My elect. Many will seek to entrap you in the turmoil that is coming.

My chosen ones will possess something the world cannot imitate—My glory. They will carry an anointing through the world the enemy will attempt to stop, but he is unable, for My mighty angels shall protect you as you go from place to place to place witnessing of Me in this time.

Know as the days grow darker, so does My Spirit grow brighter within those who are truly Mine. You will know them by this—by My Spirit shining brightly through them. You will know them, for they shall possess My love for all mankind and sacrificially so, for they love not their own lives. They love not the world around them. Their hearts long to be here with Me, and so shall they all be very soon. Very soon indeed.

My love abides in you, My children. My love flows to you and through you to others that you may witness of My great love for all mankind. My heart grieves over the sin in the world, and I must purge it. I must purge My holy bride of all sin. She must be pure and holy before Me.

I desire that each of My chosen ones would stand ready at their post, ready to receive My instructions for what each of you are to do for Me in this time. I desire you to be watching and praying—praying for this sinful world, praying you will not enter into temptation, praying for the lost, that I would save them before it is too late, which it soon will be for many. I desire to find you watching—hopeful of My Son's return, waiting on your Bridegroom.

When catastrophe strikes near you, many of you will feel as if the end of the world is already here, but it is not yet. Not yet, but not far off either. It will seem so to many of you as you watch your world—the world as you know it—come crashing down around you. Stand fast, My children, for these things must happen before My Son's return. Stand fast and stand ready. Ready for My commands to you to do all I have called each of you to do in this time.

Each of you shall play an important role. Oh yes, many of you think "Lord, what could I possibly be used for?" But I have a role for each of you to play, and you shall influence souls for Me. Be quick to obey Me when I call you, for there is little time left in which to act before all is lost for so many in this world.

MY CHILDREN, THE FULL SCOPE OF WHAT IS COMING TO THE WORLD IS FAR WORSE THAN THE SCENARIOS YOU HAVE IMAGINED. Man's mind cannot fully comprehend the pure evil planned for you by the enemy, but I have already made provision for your protection. LEGIONS OF ANGELS ARE BEING SENT TO GUARD MY CHOSEN ONES IN THIS TIME. You will be surrounded by angels on every side who fight for you, assist you, minister to you. I planned this long ago, for if I did not, not one of you could endure.

Matt. 24:21-22: For then shall be great tribulation, such as was not since the beginning of the world to this time, no, nor ever shall be. And except those days should be shortened, there should no flesh be saved: but for the elect's sake those days shall be shortened.

1 Peter 5:8: Be sober, be vigilant; because your adversary the devil, as a roaring lion, walketh about, seeking whom he may devour:

Isaiah 60:2: For, behold, the darkness shall cover the earth, and gross darkness the people: but the LORD shall arise upon thee, and his glory shall be seen upon thee.

John 12:25: He that loveth his life shall lose it; and he that hateth his life in this world shall keep it unto life eternal.

Eph. 5:27: That he might present it to himself a glorious church, not having spot, or wrinkle, or any such thing; but that it should be holy and without blemish.

Mark 13:33: Take ye heed, watch and pray: for ye know not when the time is.

Mark 14:38: Watch ye and pray, lest ye enter into temptation. The spirit truly is ready, but the flesh is weak.

Luke 21:36: Watch ye therefore, and pray always, that ye may be accounted worthy to escape all these things that shall come to pass, and to stand before the Son of man.

1 Peter 4:7: But the end of all things is at hand: be ye therefore sober, and watch unto prayer.

Psalm 34:7: The angel of the LORD encampeth round about them that fear him, and delivereth them.

Psalm 91:11: For he shall give his angels charge over thee, to keep thee in all thy ways.

4/28/11

THIS STORM WILL COME UPON YOU QUICKLY

I desire that you would move forward quickly in all I have assigned you, and this shall be done, for there is no longer any time to waste. The world is quickly spiraling towards the end, and all things written in My Holy Word must be fulfilled, and so they shall.

At this point, in the Spirit I saw a sky full of storm clouds. The storm clouds began moving towards each other until it looked as if they were being pulled into a fast moving spiral like a tornado forming, only faster.

The storm you see gathering shall indeed be a fierce one, and the wind and rains will beat down on the good and the evil alike. My people who have built their house on the Rock shall survive this storm, <u>even thrive during it</u>, BUT MANY OTHERS SHALL PERISH FOR LACK OF PREPARATION. They shall perish because they did not heed My warning words or obey My command to prepare. Get ready, My people, for the storm clouds are gathering.

Many elements hide in the clouds of this storm you cannot see with earthly eyes. My children with eyes to see and ears to hear will recognize these elements for what they are: signs of the end fast approaching. My children shall be watching and praying and desiring My return, while others cry in anguish and perish from the earth. My children, those who truly know Me, shall walk in the peace that passes all understanding even in the midst of the worst storm. My angels camped round about them shall protect them and keep them as evil covers the earth.

This storm will come upon you quickly, My children. Get ready, gird up your loins, secure your houses, and pray for My guidance through what lies ahead and is soon to come, for many will not be ready. LIFE AS YOU KNOW IT IS ABOUT TO CHANGE FOREVER. These things must happen before the end comes.

Gather your families, My children. Hold tight to each other, and care for each other until this storm passes, for it is a bad one. More storms are coming to the earth soon. You have not seen the last.

(I knew He was speaking about storms in the natural here. I live in Texas, and we have just come through several days of violent thunderstorm and tornado activity.)

Fierce storms of all kinds will be common occurrences in these last days, until man can find no shelter from the storms but in Me. Hide in Me. Be found in Me. I will hide you under My wings and protect you from all that is coming, My children, if only you will obey My commands and run to Me and not to the world as your provider. If you run to the world and follow your own plans, then you will not be found in Me as this storm begins, and the world must be your provider.

Those who have known Me as their helper shall be helped. THOSE WHO SERVE ME AND HONOR ME WITH ALL THEIR SUBSTANCE SHALL BE SUSTAINED. Those who ignore Me until their time of need shall be in lack.

Prepare well, My children. Prepare by looking unto Me and obeying My commands to you. OBEY ME BY BEING EXCEEDINGLY OBEDIENT, AND YOU SHALL THRIVE IN THE COMING STORM, for My desire is that you do not lack any good thing that you need.

Seek Me now, and I will guide you in preparing your houses against the coming storm. Place Me above your very lives, and I shall prosper you in it. Ignore Me, and it shall be to your own peril. You can prepare My way or man's way. Which way will you choose?

Matt. 7:24: Therefore whosoever heareth these sayings of mine, and doeth them, I will liken him unto a wise man, which built his house upon a rock.

Luke 6:48: He is like a man which built an house, and digged deep, and laid the foundation on a rock: and when the flood arose, the stream beat vehemently upon that house, and could not shake it: for it was founded upon a rock.

Matt. 7:25: And the rain descended, and the floods came, and the winds blew, and beat upon that house; and it fell not: for it was founded upon a rock.

Phil. 4:7: And the peace of God, which passeth all understanding, shall keep your hearts and minds through Christ Jesus.

Psalm 91:11: For he shall give his angels charge over thee, to keep thee in all thy ways.

2 Kings 6:16-17: And he answered, Fear not: for they that be with us are more than they that be with them. And Elisha prayed, and said, LORD, I pray thee, open his eyes, that he may see. And the LORD opened the eyes of the young man; and he saw: and, behold, the mountain was full of horses and chariots of fire round about Elisha.

Psalm 34:7: The angel of the LORD encampeth round about them that fear him, and delivereth them.

Jer. 1:17: Thou therefore gird up thy loins, and arise, and speak unto them all that I command thee: be not dismayed at their faces, lest I confound thee before them.

Prov. 31:17: She girdeth her loins with strength, and strengtheneth her arms.

Job 40:7: Gird up thy loins now like a man: I will demand of thee, and declare thou unto me.

Psalm 46:1: God is our refuge and strength, a very present help in trouble.

Psalm 46:7: The LORD of hosts is with us; the God of Jacob is our refuge. Selah.

Psalm 62:8: Trust in him at all times; ye people, pour out your heart before him: God is a refuge for us. Selah.

Psalm 91:9: Because thou hast made the LORD, which is my refuge, even the most High, thy habitation;

Psalm 91:4: He shall cover thee with his feathers, and under his wings shalt thou trust: his truth shall be thy shield and buckler.

Psalm 78:20: Behold, he smote the rock, that the waters gushed out, and the streams overflowed; can he give bread also? can he provide flesh for his people?

Psalm 30:10: Hear, O LORD, and have mercy upon me: LORD, be thou my helper.

Psalm 54:4: Behold, God is mine helper: the Lord is with them that uphold my soul.

5/01/11

YOU CANNOT LOVE THE WORLD AND LOVE ME

I will give you revelation as you study My Holy Word. I desire that you would come into the knowledge of all truth about Me and that it will comfort you in your time of need. My Word is your assurance I will meet those needs if you have obeyed My commands.

My Word abounds with revelation, with truth, with the steps you should take in order to come out of any negative situation you are faced with; but so many rely only on the revelations of others. They do not pursue truth for themselves; therefore they possess no real revelation of their own. Because of this, they can be easily swayed by winds of strange doctrines containing only partial truths.

Oh My people, why do you neglect so great a salvation as that which is found in My Holy Word? Why do you gladly give your minds to idle pastimes and neglect the great treasures of eternal value hidden in My Word? I have hidden tools there for you to find—tools to fix the problems you face each day. I have placed comfort in its lines to surround you with My comfort whenever you need Me. YOU DRAW NEAR TO ME WHENEVER YOU READ MY HOLY WORD. I speak to you in its pages. I pull you close to Me in its verses.

I long for you to draw nearer to Me. Yet so many of you are chasing what the world has to offer, and soon that world will be no more. That world will change forever, but I change not. Time spent in My Holy Word is never wasted, never lost. It is multiplied back to you in blessings in your life.

My Word teaches you how you should live, but so many of you want to live like the world instead. You do not look into My Word, for it convicts you of your sin. Instead you look into the world, and it agrees with your sin and leaves you feeling comfortable with it. I did not call you to live lives of comfort but of sacrifice and love—lives of giving, of helping each other. Yet so many of you have turned inward with your love and love yourselves instead. My Word would teach you, but you harden your hearts against it. My Word would guide you into all truth in holiness, yet you will have none of it.

The time is coming soon when those who have spent time in My Word will stand above the others who have played the harlot with the world and its ways. The difference will be clear in the way I protect them from all that is coming soon. I have called you to come out of the world. If you ignore My voice, if you ignore My Word, you cannot endure to the end. You cannot love the world and love Me. You cannot serve the ways of the world and serve Me. You must choose.

Prov. 1:23: Turn you at my reproof: behold, I will pour out my Spirit unto you, I will make known my words unto you.

Isaiah 28:9: Whom shall he teach knowledge? and whom shall he make to understand doctrine? them that are weaned from the milk, and drawn from the breasts.

Eph. 4:14: That we henceforth be no more children, tossed to and fro, and carried about with every wind of doctrine, by the sleight of men, and cunning craftiness, whereby they lie in wait to deceive.

1 Tim. 4:1: Now the Spirit speaketh expressly, that in the latter times some shall depart from the faith, giving heed to seducing spirits, and doctrines of devils;

2 Tim. 4:3: For the time will come when they will not endure sound doctrine; but after their own lusts shall they heap to themselves teachers, having itching ears.

Hebrews 2:3: How shall we escape, if we neglect so great salvation; which at the first began to be spoken by the Lord, and was confirmed unto us by them that heard him.

Malachi 3:6: For I am the LORD, I change not; therefore ye sons of Jacob are not consumed.

Ezekiel 16:49: hold, this was the iniquity of thy sister Sodom, pride, fulness of bread, and abundance of idleness was in her and in her daughters, neither did she strengthen the hand of the poor and needy.

Prov. 2:3-5: Yea, if thou criest after knowledge, and liftest up thy voice for understanding; If thou seekest her as silver, and searchest for her as for hid treasures; Then shalt thou understand the fear of the LORD, and find the knowledge of God.

Isaiah 45:3: And I will give thee the treasures of darkness, and hidden riches of secret places, that thou mayest know that I, the LORD, which call thee by thy name, am the God of Israel.

Romans 15:4: For whatsoever things were written aforetime were written for our learning, that we through patience and comfort of the scriptures might have hope.

2 Cor. 1:3: Blessed be God, even the Father of our Lord Jesus Christ, the Father of mercies, and the God of all comfort.

James 4:8: Draw nigh to God, and he will draw nigh to you. Cleanse your hands, ye sinners; and purify your hearts, ye double minded.

John 6:63: It is the Spirit that quickeneth; the flesh profiteth nothing: the words that I speak unto you, they are spirit, and they are life.

John 3:19: And this is the condemnation, that light is come into the world, and men loved darkness rather than light, because their deeds were evil.

Hosea 4:6: My people are destroyed for lack of knowledge: because thou hast rejected knowledge, I will also reject thee, that thou shalt be no priest to me: seeing thou hast forgotten the law of thy God, I will also forget thy children.

5/07/11

DESTRUCTION IS COMING TO AMERICA

This impression and Word came to me on the fourth day of a ten day fast. I was outside and glanced slightly northeast of north from the town where I live in Texas, just north of the Dallas area.

Suddenly a feeling of black mass destruction coming somewhere to the north or northeast stopped me in my tracks. It was so massive and so deadly, all I could do was stand and stare in that direction. It felt like a huge black cloud of death hovering unseen above its intended target.

I want to clarify why I felt this impression was important, because I don't know what the dark cloud was that I sensed, but the feeling I got and the way it stopped me in my tracks is something I have only experienced once before.

The one other time it happened, I was out on a job in North Texas and was busy running to and fro doing what I had been hired to do. I really wasn't focused on receiving prophetic impressions or Words at that time. On that day, I noticed an airplane flying over and for some reason that I could not explain, I could not stop staring at it. I had this strange feeling in my spirit that I could not define, but I knew something significant was coming that involved airplanes. The next morning—on 9/11—something significant did happen!

Often those with a prophetic anointing sense impressions they do not know how to interpret, and because we all know in part and prophesy in part (1 Cor. 13:9), if we all share what we have seen, we can put the pieces together and get a clearer picture of what is coming, because the Lord is giving other parts to other believers.

Afterwards, I began praying in the Spirit, asking the Lord to speak to me about what I had felt in the Spirit. This is the message He gave me.

Why do you settle for less, My people? Why are you so willing to accept less than the best I have for you in this time? This is the time of great blessing, of great harvest, of all I have been holding back for you, and yet still you are willing to be content with so much less than I have for you. Are you so small in your own eyes or am I?

Now is the time of miracles, of the great and mighty signs and wonders My Son spoke about in My Word. In this time you shall do greater works than even those of My Son while He was on the earth.

Yes, destruction is coming to America. Destruction must come. I must tear down before I can build up again that which was lost in unrighteousness. We must build again in holiness and what is right in My eyes, not the impurities that now exist. What is coming will be black and deadly, and it will show no mercy; and yet, unless it comes, I cannot show mercy to those who are left to rebuild, for I cannot bless this sinful nation any longer. You are filled with abominations and whoredoms. Unrighteousness fills your homes and runs through the streets of every city in this nation. My people are content with the filth that abounds here, and this is an abomination to Me.

My gospel is a gospel of righteousness, of holiness, not of tolerance of evil and wickedness. Why do you call evil good, My people? How is it that you do not see it for what it is? If you looked into My Word as I have told you time and time again, you would recognize sinfulness when you encounter it, but you prefer the lies of this sinful world to the truth found in My Holy Word.

Those who repent on behalf of this nation shall be saved. I shall show mercy to them, but for others who ignore My Holy Word and ignore My warnings, you shall be taken in your own folly, for you care not about the things of My Kingdom. You do not care enough to seek My face.

Let destruction come. Let us build again that which is holy and righteous in My eyes.

Why do you not turn from your wicked ways and shun those who practice evil? Why do you not beg Me to cleanse you from all unrighteousness before it is too late?

At this point I saw in the Spirit that He is speaking to some of you who are reading this Word, but who will ignore it and will perish in the destruction that is coming because you love your sin too much to give it up. You love the world and its ways, but you want the Lord's blessings too. You can't have both. You must choose, my friend. We are all required to make this choice.

John 14:12: Verily, verily, I say unto you, He that believeth on me, the works that I do shall he do also; and greater works than these shall he do; because I go unto my Father.

Ezra 9:14: Should we again break thy commandments, and join in affinity with the people of these abominations? wouldest not thou be angry with us till thou hadst consumed us, so that there should be no remnant nor escaping?

Isaiah 66:3-4: He that killeth an ox is as if he slew a man; he that sacrificeth a lamb, as if he cut off a dog's neck; he that offereth an oblation, as if he offered swine's blood; he that burneth incense, as if he blessed an idol. Yea, they have chosen their own ways, and their soul delighteth in their abominations. I also will choose their delusions, and will bring their fears upon them; because when I called, none did answer; when I spake, they did not hear: but they did evil before mine eyes, and chose that in which I delighted not.

Isaiah 5:20: Woe unto them that call evil good, and good evil; that put darkness for light, and light for darkness; that put bitter for sweet, and sweet for bitter!

Prov. 15:21: Folly is joy to him that is destitute of wisdom: but a man of understanding walketh uprightly.

5/23/11

AMERICA HAS BECOME THE HARLOT OF THE WORLD

I was watching a news video online showing the devastation in Joplin, Missouri from the tornadoes yesterday. Suddenly a wave of grief hit my spirit and the Lord spoke and said:

America hasn't seen anything yet.

America does not understand what it means to be under My mighty hand of judgment. For so long she has basked in her power and in her glory, when she was originally created to worship Mine. She has turned from My ways and My words and become the harlot of the world, spreading her wickedness to other nations, partaking of her sins openly and proudly. I will now destroy her pridefulness. I will cast her beauty to the ground and trample it under My feet. She will have no reason for pridefulness then.

She has turned her face from My holy city Jerusalem and turned her back on My beloved Israel. I will now turn My back on her. America will pay for her treachery, for her pridefulness, for her wickedness. Her sins have come up before Me, and her cup of sin is full. My righteous anger at her sins, her abominations, her harlotry, shall be avenged.

Prepare, My people, prepare to see what I will do to this once great country, for her time of judgment is nearing with every moment. Prepare to see this great country destroyed, for I shall leave no power in her when I am done. She will not hold her head high any longer, nor lord her power over other nations when I am done judging her, but beg for help from them. I will leave her people begging in the streets and their children stricken with disease. She is no longer called by My Name.

Ezekiel 16:15: But thou didst trust in thine own beauty, and playedst the harlot because of thy renown, and pouredst out they fornications on every one that passed by; his it was.

Nahum 3:4-5: Because of the multitude of thy whoredoms of the well favoured harlot, the mistress of witchcrafts, that selleth nations through her whoredoms, and families through her witchcrafts. Behold, I am against thee, saith the Lord of Hosts; and I will discover thy skirts upon thy face, and I will show the nations thy nakedness, and the kingdoms thy shame.

Hosea 4:7: As they were increased, so they sinned against Me; therefore will I change their glory into shame.

Proverbs 16:18: Pride goeth before destruction, and an haughty spirit before a fall.

5/27/11

I DESIRE MY PEOPLE WOULD PREPARE

My people have become steeped in complacency. Most hear My Word but do not heed it. They have become hearers but not doers.

MY HOLY WORD CONTAINS ALL THE POWER YOU NEED TO OVERCOME IN ANY SITUATION.

I desire that My people would prepare for what is coming, but many are running to and fro in the earth concerned about worldly matters. They do not heed My words of warning in the earth, though time is short now. They prefer the pleasures of the world to spending time in My presence.

James 1:22: But be ye doers of the Word, and not hearers only, deceiving your own selves.

Jeremiah 6:10: To whom shall I speak, and give warning, that they may hear? Behold, their ear is uncircumcised, and they cannot hearken; behold, the Word of the Lord is unto them a reproach; they have no delight in it.

6/05/11

WHEN WILL YOU HEED MY WORDS?

I desire My people would see Me as their provision and provider. I desire you would not walk in fear but rely on the truth found in My Word that I shall supply all your needs according to My riches in glory which are very great.

When you doubt My provision, you doubt My love for you. If you have been obedient to My commands and obeyed all I have spoken to you, what is there to fear?

I truly will make a way for you in all that is coming to the earth. SOME OF YOU I WILL SPEAK TO, TO MOVE TO OTHER PLACES, AND SOME I WILL PROVIDE FOR WHERE YOU ARE. If you obey Me, the provision will appear. Concern yourselves with obedience to My Word and listening to My voice.

Things are about to get much worse in the world, for one is coming soon who will cause this. He is from the enemy's camp, and there is nothing you can do to stop him. But be aware, My children, that I see and know all things, and I shall fiercely protect those of you who are Mine.

I saw the tall dark form of a man, but could not see any of his features because he was in the shadows. I sensed great darkness and evil, that his intentions are very evil. The Lord did not tell me if he is anyone spoken about in Revelations, and I could not see any other details about him, but I do feel he is a leader of some kind, possibly a government leader. I was not shown his nationality, where he was, what country he is from, or the time frame in which he will be revealed.

I shall increase My words to My children in coming months. Many who have never heard My voice will hear it for the first time. Know, My children, that it is My desire you hear Me speak, but you must declutter your busy lives to make room for Me if you wish to hear Me.

I will be releasing Words about events soon to come to warn those who have ears to hear. Many will turn a deaf ear and go about their worldly pursuits and will be taken in these events, but this is not My desire.

Oftentimes My children blame Me for those who do not listen and then perish. Know, My children, that I love each of you with a love you cannot even comprehend, and for this reason I do warn you, but many of you are like small rebellious children who refuse to come away from the fire. Do you not know that fire always burns? It is by its very nature hot and burning, and yet you return again and again to the sin that burns you in the end. You ignore My words of coming disasters and continue playing by the fire, even after hearing My words of warning.

What is coming is a very great disaster, and many lives will be lost. Many souls will perish in that time. I desire they would be saved, and I have sent My words to them, but they are refusing My instruction, and the loss will be very great. Many shall mourn in that time: mourn the loss of loved ones, the loss of property, the huge blow to your economy this shall bring.

When will you heed My words to you, My children? When will you hear and understand that I love you, and I desire you would turn from your wickedness and be saved from your sins? When will you see how great My love is and how many times I have saved you from yourselves, how I have preserved your lives to give you one more chance to hear Me and obey Me? When will you receive Me? When will you make Me your God and throw down those false gods you are worshiping now? How I long for you to pursue Me instead of them!

(I could hear great sadness in the Lord's voice when He spoke this last sentence.)

Many disasters are soon to strike the world. Some will be man-made, but many will blame Me for them. Some of them are even planned. Yes, My people, there are those in the world who will harm you for their own motives.

Seek Me for understanding and wisdom. I will guide you in the times to come.

Philippians 4:19: But my God shall supply all your need according to his riches in glory by Christ Jesus.

Matthew 4:4: But he answered and said, It is written, Man shall not live by bread alone, but by every Word that proceedeth out of the mouth of God.

Matthew 6:28-29: And why take ye thought for raiment? Consider the lilies of the field, how they grow; they toil not, neither do they spin: And yet I say unto you, That even Solomon in all his glory was not arrayed like one of these.

Genesis 12:1: Now the LORD had said unto Abram, Get thee out of thy country, and from thy kindred, and from thy father's house, unto a land that I will shew thee.

John 3:16: For God so loved the world, that he gave his only begotten Son, that whosoever believeth in him should not perish, but have everlasting life.

2 Peter 3:9: The Lord is not slack concerning his promise, as some men count slackness; but is longsuffering to us-ward, not willing that any should perish, but that all should come to repentance.

Isaiah2:8: Their land also is full of idols; they worship the work of their own hands, that which their own fingers have made.

Proverbs 2:6: For the LORD giveth wisdom: out of his mouth cometh knowledge and understanding.

Proverbs 9:10: The fear of the LORD is the beginning of wisdom: and the knowledge of the holy is understanding.

Psalm 91
1. He that dwelleth in the secret place of the most High shall abide under the shadow of the Almighty.
2. I will say of the LORD, He is my refuge and my fortress: my God; in him will I trust.
3. Surely he shall deliver thee from the snare of the fowler, and from the noisome pestilence.
4. He shall cover thee with his feathers, and under his wings shalt thou trust: his truth shall be thy shield and buckler.
5. Thou shalt not be afraid for the terror by night; nor for the arrow that flieth by day;
6. Nor for the pestilence that walketh in darkness; nor for the destruction that wasteth at noonday.

7. A thousand shall fall at thy side, and ten thousand at thy right hand; but it shall not come nigh thee.

8. Only with thine eyes shalt thou behold and see the reward of the wicked.

9. Because thou hast made the LORD, which is my refuge, even the most High, thy habitation;

10. There shall no evil befall thee, neither shall any plague come nigh thy dwelling.

11. For he shall give his angels charge over thee, to keep thee in all thy ways.

12. They shall bear thee up in their hands, lest thou dash thy foot against a stone.

13. Thou shalt tread upon the lion and adder: the young lion and the dragon shalt thou trample under feet.

14. Because he hath set his love upon me, therefore will I deliver him: I will set him on high, because he hath known my name.

15. He shall call upon me, and I will answer him: I will be with him in trouble; I will deliver him, and honour him.

16. With long life will I satisfy him, and shew him my salvation.

6/09/11

THERE SHALL BE WEEPING AND MOURNING IN AMERICA

I was praying and asking the Lord if He had any Word for the people for Thursday night's Blog Talk program. This was His response.

Indeed I do have a Word for you, My child, and for all My people and those who are not yet Mine.

Tell them I love them with a love that won't die. I am the One who will never leave them, never be untrue. I long to see them living happy, fulfilled lives, not lives filled with empty fleeting pleasures. I long for them to be found in Me during the coming storm so I can protect them, provide for them, and keep them safe from harm; but so many see Me as weak or cruel because they have no understanding.

They have settled for the wisdom of the world instead of seeking My wisdom. They have built for themselves strong houses of refuge which they think will protect them from disaster, but they are mistaken, for they know not what disasters I have in store for those who deny Me, and their strong houses will not save them.

This wealth will not protect them nor shall their wisdom deliver them from My mighty hand, for I see the plans they have made and the wickedness in their hearts.

They have set themselves up gods that cannot save. They have made themselves into the gods of this world, but I shall show them in that time that they are no gods at all, but weak and feeble and ignorant of true wisdom. They shall find themselves lacking in that time, and who will protect them then? Who shall save you from My mighty Hand of Judgment, oh foolish man?

They shall be trapped in their own snares in that time, and great shall be the destruction that falls on them then. I will that they would turn to Me and be saved and not perish, but they refuse to hear Me and turn from their wickedness.

WOE TO THOSE who are wise in their own sight, for I shall bring their wisdom to nothing before their eyes.

WOE TO THEM who devise wicked schemes against My people for their own gain, for they shall not escape My mighty Hand of Judgment at all.

WOE TO THEM who refuse to help the poor and the helpless when they are able, for they themselves shall be in want.

Famine comes soon to the land of America. The land known for plenty shall soon lack the food to feed even her own people, for

My mighty Hand of Judgment is on this land. STORE UP, MY PEOPLE, STORE UP GRAIN TO FEED YOUR LITTLE ONES, for it shall come upon you quickly and without warning, and it is indeed coming soon. Store up My Word in your hearts, for it shall be a comfort to you in these days of sorrow.

There shall be great weeping and mourning in America, for her time is near to know My judgments. But here shall My glory also be known among My people, for in this time of great darkness My mighty power shall shine brightly among My chosen ones.

Hebrews 13:5: Let your conversation be without covetousness; and be content with such things as ye have: for he hath said, I will never leave thee, nor forsake thee.

1 John 4:15-16: Whosoever shall confess that Jesus is the Son of God, God dwelleth in him, and he in God. And we have known and believed the love that God hath to us. God is love; and he that dwelleth in love dwelleth in God, and God in him.

Job 28:12-13: But where shall wisdom be found? and where is the place of understanding? Man knoweth not the price thereof; neither is it found in the land of the living.

Job 28:28: And unto man he said, Behold, the fear of the LORD, that is wisdom; and to depart from evil is understanding.

Psalm 57:1: Be merciful unto me, O God, be merciful unto me: for my soul trusteth in thee: yea, in the shadow of thy wings will I make my refuge, until these calamities be overpast.

Psalm 49:6-7: They that trust in their wealth, and boast themselves in the multitude of their riches; None of them can by any means redeem his brother, nor give to God a ransom for him.

Proverbs 11:4: Riches profit not in the day of wrath: but righteousness delivereth from death.

Proverbs 18:10-12: The name of the LORD is a strong tower: the righteous runneth into it, and is safe. The rich man's wealth is his strong city, and as an high wall in his own conceit. Before destruction the heart of man is haughty, and before honour is humility.

Jeremiah 2:28: But where are thy gods that thou hast made thee? let them arise, if they can save thee in the time of thy trouble: for according to the number of thy cities are thy gods, O Judah.

Jeremiah 11:12: Then shall the cities of Judah and inhabitants of Jerusalem go, and cry unto the gods unto whom they offer incense: but they shall not save them at all in the time of their trouble.

6/17/11

I AM RAISING UP SOME OF YOU TO LEAD THE WAY

I was praying about the confusion some have expressed over storing food versus not storing food etc. and for what the Lord has to say to His people in the radio program this week, and this is what He gave me.

I desire My people would be fully ready for what is soon to come. I desire they would not be caught unaware as the world shall be. The world does not hear Me, but you, My people, do hear My voice, and I desire you would hear Me even more than you do.

My people, your natural minds tell you to store up and make refuge, yet you know not what is in store, so how can you? Yes, I have spoken to some of you and through My prophets, but there is more coming you know not of.

I DESIRE YOU WOULD SEEK ME, THAT I MAY GUIDE YOU INTO PERSONAL PREPARATIONS FOR YOURSELF AND YOUR LOVED ONES. ONLY I KNOW WHICH PROVISIONS WILL BE OF BENEFIT AND HOW SOON YOU WILL NEED THEM.

Some of you are running to and fro seeking Words when I desire you would seek Me, the giver of the Words. Why seek ye Words and not the One who speaks them, when I am so accessible to you? Why is it you trust man more than Me, the Creator of man? You are walking by sight and this is not of faith.

I am raising up some of you to guide others in how to walk by faith in the times soon to come. You will lead the way, that others may know Me better.

Learn, My children, learn to trust Me for everything, for the day is coming when you must do this to survive. Study the miracles of My mighty power in My Holy Word that you may better understand My ways and how to receive provision. Know that I will make a way of escape for those of you who will need one. Spend your time girding up your loins and feasting on My Word in preparation to run this race.

At this point I felt strongly that storing up food etc. was not wrong, nor is the Lord against it, but He does not want all our faith to be in our stored provisions. He does not want us to ultimately trust in our provisions to save us from what is coming, but in Him.

I feel He is saying to know His Word and thus know Him and walk close to Him, so we can be led by Him. I don't think He wants us to be careless and carefree like grasshoppers, but to be wise like ants. But most of all and more important than storing food, He wants us to draw close to Him and to hear from Him and to be sharpening our swords so that we are ready to slay any giants that may come our way.

6/20/11

REPENT WHILE THERE IS STILL TIME

Repent!

Repent, My people, while there is still time left for you. Many of you hear My words and the messages I send through My prophets, and laugh, but I say this to you now: You will not laugh when My judgments fall on your land, but tremble in fear.

It is not My desire that you perish. It is not My desire that you walk in hardship, yet you refuse to turn when I call you. You refuse and pretend you do not hear.

Do you not know I see the wickedness in your hearts? Do you not know you can hide nothing from Me? Turn your hearts to Me while there is still time.

Joel 2:12-13: Therefore also now, saith the LORD, turn ye even to me with all your heart, and with fasting, and with weeping, and with mourning: And rend your heart, and not your garments, and turn unto the LORD your God: for he is gracious and merciful, slow to anger, and of great kindness, and repenteth him of the evil.

Matthew 4:17: From that time Jesus began to preach, and to say, Repent: for the kingdom of heaven is at hand.

2 Chronicles 36:16: But they mocked the messengers of God, and despised his words, and misused his prophets, until the wrath of the LORD arose against his people, till there was no remedy.

Amos 3:7: Surely the Lord GOD will do nothing, but he revealeth his secret unto his servants the prophets.

Proverbs 19:29: Judgments are prepared for scorners, and stripes for the back of fools.

Jude 1:17-19: But, beloved, remember ye the words which were spoken before of the apostles of our Lord Jesus Christ; How that they told you there should be mockers in the last time, who should walk after their own ungodly lusts. These be they who separate themselves, sensual, having not the Spirit.

Matthew 18:14: Even so it is not the will of your Father which is in heaven, that one of these little ones should perish.

Genesis 6:5: And God saw that the wickedness of man was great in the earth, and that every imagination of the thoughts of his heart was only evil continually.

Proverbs 1:24-31: Because I have called, and ye refused; I have stretched out my hand, and no man regarded; But ye have set at nought all my counsel, and would none of my reproof: I also will laugh at your calamity; I will mock when your fear cometh; When your fear cometh as desolation, and your destruction cometh as a whirlwind; when distress and anguish cometh upon you. Then shall they call upon me, but I will not answer; they shall seek me early, but they shall not find me: For that they hated knowledge, and did not choose the fear of the LORD: They would none of my counsel: they despised all my reproof. Therefore shall they eat of the fruit of their own way, and be filled with their own devices.

6/23/11

LET THE DIVIDING LINES BE DRAWN

I heard from a friend that TBN was pulling Jack Van Impe's programming because of his criticism of "Chrislam." I was praying about it when the Lord brought to my remembrance something He had shown me a few months ago during prayer—that there is corruption in TBN which will be exposed, and DayStar will take TBN's place in the rankings of Christian networks.

Let the dividing lines be drawn. I will now bring situations into each believer's life to cause them to choose. You must decide now, My children, whether you will truly serve Me, the Holy One of Israel, or the god of this world.

For those of you in love with this world, you shall go the way of the world and reap the fruits thereof, but My children will choose righteously. Those who are called by My Name and walk in My ways will choose to serve Me no matter the cost, and they shall be greatly rewarded in times to come. They shall be strengthened for what is coming. I shall be the lifter of their heads, their strong tower. They shall run in to Me and be safe from harm.

But woe unto you who choose to serve the god of this world, for it would be better for you if you had never been born. What awaits you is terrible indeed.

Think on this: I am raising up a standard. Choose you this day whom you will serve.

Amos 7:7: Thus he showed me: and, behold, the LORD stood upon a wall made by a plumbline, with a plumbline in his hand.

Joshua 24:15: And if it seem evil unto you to serve the LORD, choose you this day whom ye will serve; whether the gods which your fathers served that were on the other side of the flood, or the gods of the Amorites, in whose land ye dwell: but as for me and my house, we will serve the LORD.

Hosea 10:12-13: Sow to yourselves in righteousness, reap in mercy; break up your fallow ground: for it is time to seek the LORD, till he come and rain righteousness upon you. Ye have plowed wickedness, ye have reaped iniquity; ye have eaten the fruit of lies: because thou didst trust in thy way, in the multitude of thy mighty men.

Psalm 3:3: But thou, O LORD, art a shield for me; my glory, and the lifter up of mine head.

Psalm 61:3: For thou hast been a shelter for me, and a strong tower from the enemy.

Proverbs 18:10: The name of the LORD is a strong tower: the righteous runneth into it, and is safe.

Isaiah 59:18-19: According to their deeds, accordingly he will repay, fury to his adversaries, recompence to his enemies; to the islands he will repay recompence. So shall they fear the name of the LORD from the west, and his glory from the rising of the sun. When the enemy shall come in like a flood, the Spirit of the LORD shall lift up a standard against him.

6/26/11

WHY DO YOU SAY YOU ARE MINE?

I have many Words to tell My people, that they may prepare and be ready for what is coming, that they may not be caught unaware, as the world shall, for the coming of the Evil One.

My people perish for lack of knowledge, yet they fill their lives with everything of the world and so little that is of Me or My Word. Their televisions carry filth, and yet they take it in night after night, filling themselves with sinful thoughts and worldly pleasures, and this is not of Me. I am not at all pleased with this.

Why do you say you are Mine and saturate yourselves with the stain of this world? Do you not know? Do you not see that this displeases Me? That the enemy is gaining more access to your life through doors you open to him? Do you not understand that I am holy? Do you not see how his ways contaminate your thinking and thus your behavior?

Do not be deceived, little ones, into thinking I do not see or care when you avail yourselves of worldly entertainment and worldly pleasures, when your thoughts are filled with sin and lust and greed and murder.

Why are you not preparing in My Word for what is coming? Why do you waste precious hours and days delving into the world when so much is at stake? Do you not think you will give account to Me for what you have done and all you have left undone? AS YOUR MIND BECOMES FILLED WITH THE WORLD, SO YOUR CONVERSATION FOLLOWS AND YOUR ACTIONS. You look and act like the world, My children, and this is not pleasing to Me at all.

I desire you would spend more time in My presence, time away from the world and its filth for it is contaminated by the Evil One and is the path to destruction.

How I long for you to think on Me and My Word and follow in My ways, but you have turned aside to another whose intent is to destroy you.

Come back to Me so I can keep you safe, so I can hide you from the coming evil, SO I CAN FEED YOU IN TIMES OF FAMINE and speak comforting Words to you, so you will not fear what you are about to see.

Hosea 4:6: My people are destroyed for lack of knowledge: because thou hast rejected knowledge, I will also reject thee, that thou shalt be no priest to me: seeing thou hast forgotten the law of thy God, I will also forget thy children.

1 Peter 5:8: Be sober, be vigilant; because your adversary the devil, as a roaring lion, walketh about, seeking whom he may devour:

1 John 2:15-17: Love not the world, neither the things that are in the world. If any man love the world, the love of the Father is not in him. For all that is in the world, the lust of the flesh, and the lust of the eyes, and the pride of life, is not of the Father, but is of the world. And the world passeth away, and the lust thereof: but he that doeth the will of God abideth for ever.

Proverbs 4:23-24: Keep thy heart with all diligence; for out of it are the issues of life. Put away from thee a froward mouth, and perverse lips put far from thee.

Matthew 7:13: Enter ye in at the strait gate: for wide is the gate, and broad is the way, that leadeth to destruction, and many there be which go in thereat:

Joshua 1:8: This book of the law shall not depart out of thy mouth; but thou shalt meditate therein day and night, that thou mayest observe to do according to all that is written therein: for then thou shalt make thy way prosperous, and then thou shalt have good success.

John 10:10: The thief cometh not, but for to steal, and to kill, and to destroy: I am come that they might have life, and that they might have it more abundantly.

6/28/11

REND YOUR HEARTS TO ME

Come unto Me, My people. Let Me make you clean again in My eyes. Let Me wash you clean from the filth of the world you abide in. I desire you would abide in Me, the Most Holy, the Holy One of Israel. I desire you to walk clean of that which surrounds you, free of its pressure to conform to its image. I desire you to be like Me.

If you will only yield yourselves as instruments of My righteous-ness, I will perform miracles in your lives! Many of you have asked Me for a miracle, yet you go about with the stain of the world on you and do not even attempt to get free of the influence of the Evil One.

At this point in His speaking, I heard great sadness in the Lord's voice. It was obvious our sin makes Him very, very sad.

You desire his ways more than Mine, yet you ask Me to bless you. This cannot be, My children, for My blessings come with obedience to My Word and walking in My ways before Me.

In times soon to come, many of you will feel My mighty hand of judgment upon your lives. I desire you would repent before Me—repent now of allowing the world to embrace you. Repent for embracing it back. Though you are in it, I desire you would not be of it and that you would not desire it, and yet you do. Many of you still love the world and its ways more than you love Me and Mine.

Turn. Turn now at My reproof, that you may be saved from what otherwise awaits you. Turn now and rend your hearts to Me that I may spare you from these terrible judgments about to be poured out on all nations. Turn now and give Me all areas of your lives, not just one or two. Give Me your hearts in earnest, not holding back and calling yourselves by My holy name. Become truly Mine in all areas that I may spare you.

Walk holy before Me and before those around you that they may see Me and know Me through you. Do you not know this is part of your witness for Me? Do you not see that you cannot serve the world and your own desires and also Me? Do you not see the contradiction between your own words and actions? For I surely see it, My precious ones, and say it should not be.

Come to Me. Rend your hearts to Me and become truly Mine before it is too late.

Psalm 51:2: Wash me thoroughly from mine iniquity, and cleanse me from my sin.

Isaiah 1:16: Wash you, make you clean; put away the evil of your doings from before mine eyes; cease to do evil.

Romans 6:13: Neither yield ye your members as instruments of unrighteousness unto sin: but yield yourselves unto God, as those that are alive from the dead, and your members as instruments of righteousness unto God.

Deut. 11:26-27: Behold, I set before you this day a blessing and a curse; A blessing, if ye obey the commandments of the LORD your God, which I command you this day.

Jer. 7:23: but this thing commanded I them, saying, Obey my voice, and I will be your God, and ye shall be my people: and walk ye in all the ways that I have commanded you, that it may be well unto you.

Prov. 16:7: When a man's ways please the LORD, he maketh even his enemies to be at peace with him.

James 1:25: But whoso looketh into the perfect law of liberty, and continueth therein, he being not a forgetful hearer, but a doer of the work, this man shall be blessed in his deed.

Romans 12:2: And be not conformed to this world: but be ye transformed by the renewing of your mind, that ye may prove what is that good, and acceptable, and perfect, will of God.

1 John 2:15: Love not the world, neither the things that are in the world. If any man love the world, the love of the Father is not in him.

Prov. 1:23: Turn you at my reproof: behold, I will pour out my spirit unto you, I will make known my words unto you.

Joel 2:13: And rend your heart, and not your garments, and turn unto the LORD your God: for he is gracious and merciful, slow to anger, and of great kindness, and repenteth him of the evil.

Jer. 17:10: I the LORD search the heart, I try the reins, even to give every man according to his ways, and according to the fruit of his doings.

1 Peter 1:16: Because it is written, Be ye holy; for I am holy.

6/30/11

IT IS TIME TO CHOOSE

It should be apparent to My children the lateness of the hour they live in, yet so many are blinded by the riches of the world around them, blinded by earthly goals and dreams they hope to achieve—goals that have no Kingdom value at all.

Why do you seek riches in the world and ignore My eternal riches, My children? Do you not see? Do you not know all that is around you will be destroyed? Did I not say in My Holy Word to lay up for yourselves treasure in Heaven where moth and rust do not corrupt them? Yet still you seek after them with all your heart. You chase after fleeting illusions that can never be. Do you not know the Evil One has deceived you? That he has sold you a lie?

Destruction is coming to America. America has ceased to walk in My ways or honor My holy name, and I will no longer tolerate her unfaithfulness.

It is time for My children to rise up and take their places as My chosen ones. It is time My children no longer cared what the world and its people think of them. It is time for My children to operate in My glory and all the power it brings. It is time for My children to bow their wills before Me and submit to My calling in their lives, to lay aside their own plans and set their eyes on the prize that awaits them here in Heaven.

It is time to choose, My children. Will you choose Me as I have chosen you? Will you choose Me and My ways or the world? Will you follow Me and do My will, or refuse Me and side with the world?

At this point I felt a wave of terrible grief in my spirit.

Do you truly serve Me?
Do you truly love Me?
Are you jealous over My love as I am over yours?
Or am I just an afterthought to your days?—a someday God.

When you see My mighty hand of judgment moving against this nation, you will know I AM God of today.

Mark 4:19: And the cares of this world, and the deceitfulness of riches, and the lusts of other things entering in, choke the Word, and it becometh unfruitful.

Matthew 6:19-20: Lay not up for yourselves treasures upon earth, where moth and rust doth corrupt, and where thieves break through and steal: But lay up for yourselves treasures in heaven, where neither moth nor rust doth corrupt, and where thieves do not break through nor steal:

Deut. 14:2: For thou art an holy people unto the LORD thy God, and the LORD hath chosen thee to be a peculiar people unto himself, above all the nations that are upon the earth.

Joshua 24:15: And if it seem evil unto you to serve the LORD, choose you this day whom ye will serve; whether the gods which your fathers served that were on the other side of the flood, or the gods of the Amorites, in whose land ye dwell: but as for me and my house, we will serve the LORD.

Matthew 16:24: Then said Jesus unto his disciples, If any man will come after me, let him deny himself, and take up his cross, and follow me.

Deut. 6:15: (For the LORD thy God is a jealous God among you) lest the anger of the LORD thy God be kindled against thee, and destroy thee from off the face of the earth.

7/8/11

RISE UP AND FIGHT THE ENEMY

Rise up! Rise up, mighty warriors, for I am calling you to your posts! Be armed and ready to defend your King.

A war rages around you, My children, the ancient war between good and evil; and many of My people have laid down their weapons and are no longer fighting for what is right in My eyes. They have ceased to battle their own evil desires, though My Word clearly states what is evil and what is good. They allow the Evil One to run rampant in their hearts and minds, spreading lustful thoughts, malice, gossip, slander, and wicked schemes.

You are polluted by his influence, My children, and I desire you would become clean. I desire you would wash yourselves clean in the water of My Word and turn from wickedness. Renounce the ways of the enemy among you. I desire you would walk upright before Me.

A house divided cannot stand. You cannot side with the enemy some of the time and Me some of the time and win battles for Me. You must be wholly for Me and My Kingdom, or the vices of the Evil One will eventually overtake you.

Do you not see? Do you not know that he desires to destroy you through your own weaknesses? Rise up and fight him, My children! Do not allow yourselves to become his victims. Fight him with the weapon of truth—My Holy Word.

Truth and light will always overcome darkness and deception. He has deceived you into believing his is the better way when it is not. You must turn back to Me while there is still time, if I am to save you from what is to come in the earth.

Disasters of great magnitude lay ahead for those who dwell in the earth, but My children shall be protected if they listen and obey My voice, if they heed My voice of warning to them.

IF YOU REFUSE MY INSTRUCTION, YOU SHALL PERISH.

Gal. 5:16: This I say then, Walk in the Spirit, and ye shall not fulfil the lust of the flesh.

Col. 3:8: But now ye also put off all these; anger, wrath, malice, blasphemy, filthy communication out of your mouth.

Titus 3:3: For we ourselves also were sometimes foolish, disobedient, deceived, serving divers lusts and pleasures, living in malice and envy, hateful, and hating one another.

James 1:15: Then when lust hath conceived, it bringeth forth sin: and sin, when it is finished, bringeth forth death.

Prov. 10:18: He that hideth hatred with lying lips, and he that uttereth a slander, is a fool.

Prov. 6:14-19: These six things doth the LORD hate: yea, seven are an abomination unto him: A proud look, a lying tongue, and hands that shed innocent blood, An heart that deviseth wicked imaginations, feet that be swift in running to mischief, A false witness that speaketh lies, and he that soweth discord among brethren.

Ezek. 14:11: That the house of Israel may go no more astray from me, neither be polluted any more with all their transgressions; but that they may be my people, and I may be their God, saith the Lord GOD.

Mark 3:25: And if a house be divided against itself, that house cannot stand.

Psalm 84:11: For the LORD God is a sun and shield: the LORD will give grace and glory: no good thing will he withhold from them that walk uprightly.

John 10:10: The thief cometh not, but for to steal, and to kill, and to destroy: I am come that they might have life, and that they might have it more abundantly.

7/15/11

WHY DO YOU NOT WORSHIP ME?

My people have wandered far from Me in their hearts. There are few who worship Me in Spirit and in truth. Most only think they do, and this is not acceptable to Me. I desire true worship from My people. If I am your King—your Lord—why do you not worship Me?

Those who truly worship Me know no fear, for they feel My love around them at all times.

I am the God of all creation, yet many of My people treat Me as an afterthought. They do not make time for Me, and this does not please Me at all. You wonder that you do not walk in all of My blessings; yet I am not first in your minds and hearts, My children. You partake of sins regularly, and you marvel that you do not feel My presence. Your hearts are still given to sin in so many areas, and this should not be. You lash others with your words, you lie, you steal. Yet you think you should walk in My blessing as well. This cannot be, My children. I bless you in many ways in spite of your disobedience, but I desire you would repent and forsake your sins and come up higher with Me that I may bless you more abundantly.

Sin should not be found among My children. You have been given authority over all the power of the enemy, yet you continue to give in to temptation and stay mired in sin time and time again. Why do you not fight him, My children? Do you desire to wallow in filthiness?

Sin is not acceptable to Me in any form. I desire you would come up higher. I desire for you to overcome the Evil One, not cavort with him. Do you think you can battle an enemy in one area while serving him in another? Do not be double-minded, My children. Come to Me and worship Me in Spirit and in truth, and I will give you the key to your freedom. Only do not deceive yourselves any longer that you will not reap the consequences of your sin, for you surely shall.

John 4:23: But the hour cometh, and now is, when the true worshippers shall worship the Father in Spirit and in truth: for the Father seeketh such to worship him.

Matt. 15:8: This people draweth nigh unto me with their mouth, and honoureth me with their lips; but their heart is far from me.

Isaiah 43:15: I am the LORD, your Holy One, the creator of Israel, your King.

Luke 10:19: Behold, I give unto you power to tread on serpents and scorpions, and over all the power of the enemy: and nothing shall by any means hurt you.

Prov. 30:12: There is a generation that are pure in their own eyes, and yet is not washed from their filthiness.

James 4:8: Draw nigh to God, and he will draw nigh to you. Cleanse your hands, ye sinners; and purify your hearts, ye double minded.

2 Peter 2:19-20: While they promise them liberty, they themselves are the servants of corruption: for of whom a man is overcome, of the same is he brought in bondage. For if after they have escaped the pollutions of the world through the knowledge of the Lord and Saviour Jesus Christ, they are again entangled therein, and overcome, the latter end is worse with them than the beginning.

7/16/11

AMERICA SHALL BOW

I was in my morning prayer time, and the Lord was speaking to me about spending more time interceding for the lost and prayer in general.

Tell My people I will be returning soon. Sooner for some than for others.

At this point as the Lord was speaking, in my spirit I saw events such as car wrecks—the kinds of things that take lives very suddenly and without warning.

My mighty hand of judgment is upon the wicked nation of America, a nation covered in filth and soaked in innocent blood, a nation whose sin is a stench in My nostrils, a nation that flaunts its abominations.

At this point in the Spirit, I saw America in the form of a cheap and tawdry looking woman, and she was beckoning with her finger. Her lips were painted brightly, and there seemed to be no virtue about her.

I shall strike it with a blow no one will forget and from which it will never fully recover.

The Lord showed me in my spirit that America had followed in Lucifer's footsteps—it has set itself up as a god to other nations.

She revels in the worship of the kings of other nations, and this I abhor! I SHALL STRIKE HER WITH FIRE AND WITH FAMINE AND WITH DISEASES, and she too shall bow before the Holy One of Israel.

Do not think you can save yourselves.

My chosen ones only will I protect from what is coming. Seek My face. I will guide you that you and your households may be saved.

Jer. 50:31-32: Behold, I am against thee, O thou most proud, saith the Lord GOD of hosts: for thy day is come, the time that I will visit thee. And the most proud shall stumble and fall, and none shall raise him up: and I will kindle a fire in his cities, and it shall devour all round about him.

Joel 2:3: A fire devoureth before them; and behind them a flame burneth: the land is as the garden of Eden before them, and behind them a desolate wilderness; yea, and nothing shall escape them.

Ezek. 14:13: Son of man, when the land sinneth against me by trespassing grievously, then will I stretch out mine hand upon it, and will break the staff of the bread thereof, and will send famine upon it, and will cut off man and beast from it:

Deut. 28:20-21: The LORD shall send upon thee cursing, vexation, and rebuke, in all that thou settest thine hand unto for to do, until thou be destroyed, and until thou perish quickly; because of the wickedness of thy doings, whereby thou hast forsaken me. The LORD shall make the pestilence cleave unto thee, until he have consumed thee from off the land, whither thou goest to possess it.

7/18/11

I DELIGHT IN YOUR TRUE WORSHIP OF ME

The Lord was speaking to me about true worship in my morning prayer time when this message came.

My people do not enter all the way in to where I am; and they walk away dissatisfied, unfulfilled, and thinking I came up short, when in reality it is their worship that falls short.

The need to worship Me is a need I placed in My people, and the world has nothing that can fill this need. Only My presence fulfills you in this way. I desire My people to draw near to My throne and worship Me—to experience My beauty and feel My holiness, to draw strength from Me. When you draw near to Me in this way, you feel My power, and you are less afraid of the enemy. You feel My love for you, and you know My protection there.

If My people will do what is right and make time to worship Me, they will not be disappointed with the results. The world will disappoint you, but My love never disappoints. My love is always perfect, always faithful. It is an everlasting love no man or woman can take away from you, My children. I delight in your true worship of Me, My children, even when your attempts are feeble. I will teach you if you will press in to Me.

MANY OF YOU GIVE UP TOO EASILY ON THE THINGS OF MY KINGDOM WHEN YOU DO NOT SEE YOUR DESIRES MANIFEST IMMEDIATELY.
You deny yourselves the greater blessing when you do this, for My Kingdom overflows with mighty blessings for those willing to spend the time to press in and truly seek Me, those who long to see My face, those who long for My voice, My presence, those who want to draw near to Me to know Me. These are My true children, and for them I have showers of blessings waiting to be released.

John 4:23: But the hour cometh, and now is, when the true worshippers shall worship the Father in Spirit and in truth: for the Father seeketh such to worship him.

Psalm 73:28: But it is good for me to draw near to God: I have put my trust in the Lord GOD, that I may declare all thy works.

James 4:8: Draw nigh to God, and he will draw nigh to you. Cleanse your hands, ye sinners; and purify your hearts, ye double minded.

7/19/11

DRAW NEAR TO ME NOW

Events are soon to happen that will change the world forever. These things must come, that Scripture may be fulfilled; but My bride has not readied herself for the marriage feast, and I desire she would turn now from the sins that so easily beset her and draw near to Me in the secret place.

The days of great darkness are beginning soon, and the inhabitants of earth shall mourn for My presence. My chosen ones, My true bride, shall know My glory in that time. They shall not dwell in spiritual darkness or terror, but in My holy presence surrounded by My love and mercy and peace.

I shall shelter you in the shadow of My mighty wings, My bride. Do not fear. You shall lack no good thing in that time as you draw near to Me; but know this: Those who do not draw near to Me in this time will not have an easy time of it. They shall run to and fro in the earth looking for help, for they shall be ignorant of My power to protect them.

Do not leave the most important thing undone, My children. Draw near to Me now. Then you will understand how I will protect you then.

Hebrews 12:1: Wherefore seeing we also are compassed about with so great a cloud of witnesses, let us lay aside every weight, and the sin which doth so easily beset us, and let us run with patience the race that is set before us,

Isaiah 60:2: For, behold, the darkness shall cover the earth, and gross darkness the people: but the LORD shall arise upon thee, and his glory shall be seen upon thee.

Joel 2:1-2: Blow ye the trumpet in Zion, and sound an alarm in my holy mountain: let all the inhabitants of the land tremble: for the day of the LORD cometh, for it is nigh at hand; A day of darkness and of gloominess, a day of clouds and of thick darkness, as the morning spread upon the mountains: a great people and a strong;

there hath not been ever the like, neither shall be any more after it, even to the years of many generations.

Psalm 57:1: Be merciful unto me, O God, be merciful unto me: for my soul trusteth in thee: yea, in the shadow of thy wings will I make my refuge, until these calamities be overpast.

James 4:8: Draw nigh to God, and he will draw nigh to you. Cleanse your hands, ye sinners; and purify your hearts, ye double minded.

7/20/11

MY BRIDE IS INDIFFERENT TO ME

Recently the Lord told me to study the bride. I was reading a verse from Jeremiah, and I was two lines into it when He began giving me the message that followed, which He added to over the days that followed.

Jeremiah 33:11: The voice of joy, and the voice of gladness, the voice of the bridegroom, and the voice of the bride, the voice of them that shall say, 'Praise the LORD of hosts: for the LORD is good; for his mercy endureth for ever: and of them that shall bring the sacrifice of praise into the house of the LORD. For I will cause to return the captivity of the land, as at the first, saith the LORD.

Can the bride think of anything but her Groom? Yet you think of many things that do not include Me, saith the Lord.

Where are My devoted ones, My set-apart ones, who hunger for My presence? (I felt deep sadness and grief.) *Where are those who long after and watch for My return?*

Where is the worship due My Holy Name? Where are My worshipers? Why do they sing songs of praise to the world and not to Me? (Terrible grief in His voice.)

Why, after all I do for you, do you chase after other gods, other lovers? Why is it you will bow to the opinions and desires of those around you and not bow before Me? Am I not worthy of your praise? Your worship? Your devotion? Is there not honor due My Holy Name?

As I began to pray about what He was saying, the Lord showed me a vision of a stain covered, filthy bride. She was trashy looking, not beautiful and virtuous looking—the way you would expect a bride to be. She would stop along the way to wherever she was going, distracted by the least little thing, and laugh loudly at it. Jesus passed by her, and she didn't even notice the grief-stricken look on His face. It was as if she didn't even see Him.

You see the dirty, stained condition of My bride. She is stained with the filth of the world around her. I desire for My bride to come aside with Me, but she tarries in the world instead. (I sensed the Lord had some anger at the bride's unfaithfulness.)

My bride is indifferent to Me.

In times soon to come, she shall realize the gravity of the error of her ways. She will seek Me and cry out for Me in her distress. Then she will let Me wash her clean in the water of My Holy Word. Only then will she truly see her great need of Me. For now she is content with her lover, the world, but then she shall long for Me; she shall long for My presence. She will long to feel the security of My love, and she will truly seek Me then.

How I long for you, My bride! How I long to hold you near Me, safe from all that is coming; but you would not.

Those who seek Me early shall find Me. Those who wait shall know great distress, for many shall perish in a short amount of time.

When there is nothing left for her to cling to but My Word, then will she enter in with Me. My bride abides in the world, not in Me where I desire she would be found. In Me she will find safety. In Me she will find all her needs met in My endless supply. In Me she can take refuge, but her eyes are on another—on the world—and she is polluted with gazing at evil and corruption.

I thought of how our looking at worldly television programs and movies and news reports does this to us. It fills our minds with murder and corruption and keeps our mind off of Him and His Word.

Come out of the world, My beloved. Run to Me and be safe in My arms! Run to Me where I can protect you from what is coming.

My bride must ready herself for My return. She must wash herself clean in My Holy Word. She must turn away from the ways of this world and cling to Me.

I asked the Lord why He said at first He would wash the bride, and then He said, *She must wash herself.* He showed me that either way it is Him washing her through His Word. Some of the bride will submit now and begin to clean herself up through the water of His Word. Some will come to Him later in desperation and be cleansed as He leads them into His Word and washes them. Either way, it is His power and His Word that does the washing. We do the submitting. We submit by being willing to change and be changed by the truth of His Word.

Prov. 8:17: I love them that love me; and those that seek me early shall find me.

Jer. 3:1: They say, If a man put away his wife, and she go from him, and become another man's, shall he return unto her again? Shall not that land be greatly polluted? but thou hast played the harlot with many lovers; yet return again to me, saith the Lord.

Jer. 29:13: And ye shall seek me, and find me, when ye shall search for me with all your heart.

7/23/11

I WILL SHOWER THEM IN THE MIRACULOUS

I am the Lord your God.

Do I not deserve the utmost of your time and attention? Do I not deserve the first and best from you? Why then do you only bring Me leftovers? Why do you dishonor Me in this way? Do you not fear Me?

As I began to pray about what the Lord was speaking, He told me this:

My people no longer worship Me as I desire. Teach them to come with open hearts, teachable spirits, to hold nothing back from Me. Teach them to bow before Me in worship, to totally surrender their lives to Me.

I am going to do miraculous signs and wonders for them as they believe. As they lay their sins on the altar before Me, I will change them. I will give them hearts to worship only Me. It will change their lives forever when they experience true nearness to Me—real intimacy with the King of Kings. They shall truly know My love for them then.

Breakthrough comes as My people enter into TRUE worship of their mighty King. TOO OFTEN MY PEOPLE RUSH OFF INTO THEIR BUSY LIVES AFTER PRAYING AND ASKING ME FOR THINGS, WITHOUT WAITING FOR MY RESPONSE or even truly entering in to

My holy presence where the true blessing awaits them. I desire they would come here and sup with Me—sup of My presence, soak in My love and forgiveness, partake of My healing power.

If My people will do this each day, if they will bow not only their hearts but their bodies in homage to Me, I will shower them in the miraculous. Their difficulties in life will disappear; and they will walk in joy, full of peace, and walking in My holy anointing and power. In their worship I shall speak softly to them.

Instead they read books about Me and watch television programs about Me. Why do they not come to Me? For in My presence, I will show them the secrets of My Kingdom. I will give them of the secret manna that is only found here with Me.

In My presence is fullness of joy that will go with them through their day. In My presence is all they can ever need, the answers to all their questions, all they could ever want for in this lifetime.

Seek Me and you shall find Me.

Psalm 16:11: Thou wilt show me the path of life: in thy presence is fullness of joy; at thy right hand there are pleasures for evermore.

Rev. 2:17: He that hath an ear, let him hear what the Spirit saith unto the churches; To him that overcometh will I give to eat of the hidden manna, and will give him a white stone, and in the stone a new name written, which no man knoweth saving he that receiveth it.

Deut. 4:29: But if from thence thou shalt seek the LORD thy God, thou shalt find him, if thou seek him with all thy heart and with all thy soul.

Jer. 29:13: And ye shall seek me, and find me, when ye shall search for me with all your heart.

7/26/11

YOU MUST FORGIVE

I was writing an email to someone about how unforgiveness can open the door to terrible diseases like cancer when the Lord began to speak this Word to me:

Tell My people they must forgive those who have wronged them. Tell them they must let go of offenses and injustices and trust Me to avenge them. Tell them the sins are against Me and no other; as I have forgiven you, you must forgive others.

The Lord showed me in my spirit a person in unforgiveness, and inside the person their soul looked like one giant ugly festering wound.

Anger and unforgiveness towards others have no place in My true bride. It is an offense to Me. The time of My judgments is very near, and you must forgive all that have wronged you. I will avenge your pain in ways that you cannot. I am a righteous judge.

You must forgive all who have hurt you now, as many of you will be taken home soon in ways you cannot foresee; and many you have not forgiven will also be taken. The time is now. Do not wait, as time is much shorter than you believe. It is shorter for some than for others.

You do not know My timing, though many of you claim you do. You cannot know the intricacy of My plan or times. You know in part and see in part. You have only the pieces I have chosen to reveal to you. Many of you are puffed up in your knowledge, thinking you have Me figured out, but you know not what I am about to do in your lives.

Repent! Repent of your pridefulness and vanity while you still have time. Otherwise you will stand before My throne on judgment day and answer to Me. Humble yourselves before My mighty judgments fall in your land, for then it shall be too late for so many of you.

I desire repentance. I desire intercession. I desire My people would humble themselves before Me, give themselves to prayer, to fasting, to seeking My face.

I desire you would turn from your wickedness and escape the judgment that awaits you, but so many of you are not listening. You do not think this applies to you. You feel safe because you have not discovered the truth of My Holy Word for yourselves. Dig into My Word and you shall see; I shall show you the truths My priests shun—the truths about sin and grace and salvation. I will show you what awaits you if you ask of Me. So many of you will not ask of Me because you fear My truths, and they are not convenient for you.

Woe to this wicked generation for your sins are many! Woe to those who refuse to hear My rebukes and heed My warnings, for your time is short, and you know it not; and what awaits you is far worse!

Matthew 6:15: But if ye forgive not men their trespasses, neither will your Father forgive your trespasses.

Mark 11:25: And when ye stand praying, forgive, if ye have ought against any: that your Father also which is in heaven may forgive you your trespasses.

2 Cor. 2:9-11: For to this end also did I write, that I might know the proof of you, whether ye be obedient in all things. To whom ye forgive any thing, I forgive also: for if I forgave any thing, to whom I forgave it, for your sakes forgave I it in the person of Christ; Lest Satan should get an advantage of us: for we are not ignorant of his devices.

Eph. 4:32: And be ye kind one to another, tenderhearted, forgiving one another, even as God for Christ's sake hath forgiven you.

7/28/11

HARD TIMES LIE AHEAD

Times are coming soon when your money will not buy the things you need. INDEED, MUCH OF WHAT YOU NEED TO PURCHASE WILL NOT EVEN BE AVAILABLE.

I AM MOVING SOME OF MY BRIDE TO SAFER ZONES. My judgments shall fall quickly at the appointed times, and I desire she would be safe. Much of My bride is being held back by ties to this world: worldly pursuits, yes, but also jobs, houses, relationships not ordained by Me—associations I Myself did not orchestrate, which I desire you be removed from.

It is not My desire that any should perish and yet many shall, for they shall refuse to run to Me and be safe. They shall refuse My gospel and all it offers—one last time—and perish!

Gird up your loins, My children, for hard times lie ahead. I will be with you in the hard times as I have been with you in the good. I shall walk with you through every valley and on every mountain. I love you with an everlasting love, and wherever you go, there I am also.

This walk shall not be an easy one for many, but I shall provide for My own in these times.

All that has been foretold shall come to pass soon. Many shall indeed come to know Me as Lord, but many more shall perish. You will see My judgments falling soon on whole households. Those who refuse Me shall indeed be judged.

I shall judge individuals, families, churches, and nations. No one shall escape My judgment.

Are you ready?

Phil. 4:19: But my God shall supply all your need according to his riches in glory by Christ Jesus.

2 Peter 3:9: The Lord is not slack concerning his promise, as some men count slackness; but is longsuffering to us-ward, not willing that any should perish, but that all should come to repentance.

Matt. 28:19-20: Go ye therefore, and teach all nations, baptizing them in the name of the Father, and of the Son, and of the Holy Ghost: Teaching them to observe all things whatsoever I have commanded you: and, lo, I am with you always, even unto the end of the world. Amen.

7/29/11

I AM COMING TO EVERY HOUSEHOLD

I was sitting at my computer working, praying about the seriousness of the Word I had recently received about judgment falling on households, when the Lord began speaking this Word to me:

Tell My people I am coming to visit them. I am coming to every household in every nation, and I will render according to what I find there. Those who are found faithful will receive reward. Those who are found pure will receive reward. Those who are found watching and praying for My return will receive reward.

Those who are found continuing to cavort in the world will not. Those who love the world still, shall receive the world as their just reward, for the world is at enmity with Me and My ways and My truths. The world does not honor Me or follow Me. If you choose the world as your god, then you will receive answer from it when you cry out. If you choose the world as your god, then occupy, make ready, for from there must your help come when you are in need.

My ways have not changed. My Word changes not, yet many seek to pervert My Holy Word to allow that which I do not allow. They deceive themselves into believing what is convenient for them, instead of walking in purity before Me. These shall receive their just reward in what is coming.

Great distress is soon to come upon the earth and its inhabitants. Only those walking in purity and holiness will be shielded. Those in love with the world shall receive the world's reward in times to come.

Make ready, My children. Gird up your mind with My truths, with My Holy Word. Gird up your loins and stand ready. Prepare to battle the enemy of your souls, for the fire burns hot. This race shall not be easy for you.

Some of My children have prepared well, but many of you have not prepared at all. You are full of the world and its deceptions, My children, and not My Holy Word; and you shall not survive this battle, for the world cannot save you.

Isaiah 10:3: And what will ye do in the day of visitation, and in the desolation which shall come from far? to whom will ye flee for help? and where will ye leave your glory?

Matt. 5:8: Blessed are the pure in heart: for they shall see God.

Acts 10:34: Then Peter opened his mouth, and said, Of a truth I perceive that God is no respecter of persons:

Luke 21:36: Watch ye therefore, and pray always, that ye may be accounted worthy to escape all these things that shall come to pass, and to stand before the Son of man.

Mark 13:33: Take ye heed, watch and pray: for ye know not when the time is.

James 4:4: Ye adulterers and adulteresses, know ye not that the friendship of the world is enmity with God? whosoever therefore will be a friend of the world is the enemy of God.

8/1/11

THE ENEMY HAS LULLED YOU TO SLEEP

I was reading 1 Chronicles 21 about King David when the Lord began speaking this message to me.

Where yet is My people's fear of Me? How is it they do not fear what I am about to do? You have fallen asleep, My people. THE ENEMY HAS LULLED YOUR SOULS TO SLEEP WITH THE LIE THERE IS YET TIME TO REPENT OF THE GREAT EVILS THIS COUNTRY HAS COMMITTED AGAINST ME, the Holy One of Israel.

He has lulled you to sleep in your sins in the hope you will not awaken in time that you may be saved, and of many of you this will be true, for you continue to reject My warnings to you, preferring the lies of the world in which you live. (I felt the deep sadness of the Lord when He spoke this last sentence.)

You who refuse to give up your sin, I am coming to judge you soon. Do not be deceived, My children, into thinking I do not care when you sin, for that is the enemy's thinking, not Mine. You shall reap what you are sowing if you refuse My ways.

Turn now while there is yet time and space for you to repent, for great is the magnitude of what I am about to do. Indeed, the whole world shall be shaken by it.

Fearful and mighty is the Holy One of Israel, but My people have forgotten how strong I am in battle, and fear Me not.

2 Kings 19:22: Whom hast thou reproached and blasphemed? and against whom hast thou exalted thy voice, and lifted up thine eyes on high? even against the Holy One of Israel.

Isaiah 1:4: Ah sinful nation, a people laden with iniquity, a seed of evildoers, children that are corrupters: they have forsaken the LORD, they have provoked the Holy One of Israel unto anger, they are gone away backward.

Isaiah 17:7: At that day shall a man look to his Maker, and his eyes shall have respect to the Holy One of Israel.

Judges 16:19-20: And she made him sleep upon her knees; and she called for a man, and she caused him to shave off the seven locks of his head; and she began to afflict him, and his strength went from him. And she said, The Philistines be upon thee, Samson. And he awoke out of his sleep, and said, I will go out as at other times before, and shake myself. And he wist not that the LORD was departed from him.

Prov. 6:9-11: How long wilt thou sleep, O sluggard? when wilt thou arise out of thy sleep? Yet a little sleep, a little slumber, a little folding of the hands to sleep: So shall thy poverty come as one that travelleth, and thy want as an armed man.

Ephesians 5:14-15: Wherefore he saith, Awake thou that sleepest, and arise from the dead, and Christ shall give thee light. See then that ye walk circumspectly, not as fools, but as wise,

8/4/11

I AM CALLING MY SOLDIERS TO WAR

My people need to stand ready at My beck and call in this time. I am calling My soldiers to war in the heavenlies for Me. I am calling them to free households, neighborhoods, cities, and states for Me. I am calling you to take up your weapons and war against the enemy of your souls.

Many of you are trained and ready for battle. Others are not so ready. I desire you would train those not yet ready to war alongside you in these times. Many events are coming soon that will cause changes you are not expecting.

Rise up, My people, and prepare to make war on the enemy of your souls. Prepare to battle him to free those you love from bondage. I desire My people to live free of hurts and wounds from the past.

I desire intercession from My people.

Numbers 32:27: But thy servants will pass over, every man armed for war, before the Lord to battle, as my lord saith.

2 Samuel 22:35: He teacheth my hands to war; so that a bow of steel is broken by mine arms.

Job 5:20: In famine he shall redeem thee from death: and in war from the power of the sword.

Joel 3:9: Proclaim ye this among the Gentiles; Prepare war, wake up the mighty men, let all the men of war draw near; let them come up:

8/6/11

DRAW NEAR TO ME

I was in my morning prayer time worshiping the Lord, when He began to speak this Word to me:

Do not fear, no matter what you see happening around you. The times are evil, and evil shall abound in this time, but it shall not come nigh you while I am protecting you.

Draw near to Me in the secret place, for I shall give you great wisdom to walk in this time. You cannot survive what is coming without Me. Draw near to Me and know My love for you. Know how I care for you. I shall comfort your souls here in the secret place.

Strange signs shall abound. Things are not as they appear to be. Much is happening behind the scenes you know not of. I desire you not be deceived, My children, though you live in the time of great deception. It is not possible for man to see through such great deception without My power; that is why you must draw nearer to Me.

In our intimate times together, I shall reveal much you need to know to walk in darkness. My light shall illuminate your way before you and make your way clear.

Fear not, only come to Me.

James 1:5: If any of you lack wisdom, let him ask of God, that giveth to all men liberally, and upbraideth not; and it shall be given him.

2 Timothy 3:13: But evil men and seducers shall wax worse and worse, deceiving, and being deceived.

Psalm 91:1: He that dwelleth in the secret place of the most High shall abide under the shadow of the Almighty.

Psalm 119:105: Thy Word is a lamp unto my feet, and a light unto my path.

8/19/11

PREPARE YOUR HEARTS FOR WHAT I AM ABOUT TO DO

I was driving across a bridge over a small area of a nearby lake and was really concerned about how fast the water was evaporating. It looked more like an oversized mud puddle than a lake now, with trees sticking up everywhere. I began to pray, "Lord, the lake is drying up! The animals will die if they can't find water!" and the Lord began to speak to me about what I was seeing.

Get used to seeing death and destruction all around you, child, for My judgments are falling on this nation, and many of them will seem harsh, but I am a righteous judge. This nation has not begun to see what I have in store for those who turn their backs on My Son, My Word, and My ways. Its judgment will be horrific indeed. Yet I will save many, for I am as great in mercy as I am in judgment.

Prepare your hearts, My children, for what I am about to do. You will not like what you see, yet it is necessary that I judge the sin and rebellion I have found in your nations.

For I shall reward to each nation, each household, and each person according to what I find. I am not slack concerning My judgments, and you have had much time to repent.

Watch for Me and pray you will be counted worthy, for I am coming soon.

Prov. 13:13: Whoso despiseth the Word shall be destroyed: but he that feareth the commandment shall be rewarded.

Hosea 4:9: And there shall be, like people, like priest: and I will punish them for their ways, and reward them their doings.

Luke 21:36: Watch ye therefore, and pray always, that ye may be accounted worthy to escape all these things that shall come to pass, and to stand before the Son of man.

1 Peter 4:7: But the end of all things is at hand: be ye therefore sober, and watch unto prayer.

8/20/11

IT WILL BE A TIME AS NONE BEFORE IT

I was working on writing, and the heaviness and dread I've been feeling for weeks now about the economy rose up in my spirit once again. I have learned when I have repeated bouts of something like this, it is an indication that something is about to happen that the Lord wants to let us know about, so I went aside to my place of prayer to seek Him about it.

Times are indeed about to become more than difficult for many people.

I heard a deep, deep sadness in the Lord's voice as He spoke this to me, and I felt that He has tried to prepare many who would not listen and obey about what they need to do before this time is upon us.

You will hear of many suicides in the future—suicides of ones who could not part with their wealthy lifestyles. It will be a time as none before it. The devastation will be great, but many shall turn their hearts to Me in this time and come to know Me, and I shall help them.

Tell My children to keep their eyes on Me and follow where I guide them, and they shall be provided for in this time. DECREASE NEEDS NOW AND LEARN TO LIVE MORE SIMPLY, AND YOU SHALL HAVE LESS DISTRESS WHEN YOU SEE THIS HAPPENING, MY CHILDREN.

The world's system must come crashing down if My people are to truly return to Me while there is yet time.

I have much to show the world in this time. I have much to teach you also, My children, about My ways, about My provision.

Come to Me now. Seek My face and know Me as your Provider.

Matt. 6:28: And why take ye thought for raiment? Consider the lilies of the field, how they grow; they toil not, neither do they spin:

Phil. 4:19: But my God shall supply all your need according to his riches in glory by Christ Jesus.

8/24/11

CRY OUT TO ME

I was in my usual morning time of prayer and worship when the Lord began to speak to me.

Truly I tell you, times in the earth have increased in sorrow, and more is coming soon. For the people of the earth will know I am a Mighty God of Judgment at the end of times.

Cry out, cry out to Me for your children and your loved ones while there is yet time! Cry out for your nations that I may touch them and bring repentance! Cry out for your own souls. Pray that you will be counted worthy to escape all that is coming in the earth, for the horror of it shall indeed be great.

Many will die of starvation, and in countries where hunger is rare. Many shall die in plagues. Many shall die in vain trying to save earthly possessions. Many shall die fighting.

In my spirit I was shown a strange sight: I saw many thousands of people, and most of them had blinders on, like the blinders horses wear. They were looking straight ahead of where they were walking—smiling, expecting conditions in the world to improve, and refusing to hear any warnings. I saw the enemy coming up behind first this one, then that one, to ambush them. They never saw him coming. They were just walking through their lives waiting for everything to improve.

Luke 21:36: Watch ye therefore, and pray always, that ye may be accounted worthy to escape all these things that shall come to pass, and to stand before the Son of man.

Rev. 6: 8: And I looked, and behold a pale horse: and his name that sat on him was Death, and Hell followed with him. And power was given unto them over the fourth part of the earth, to kill with sword, and with hunger, and with death, and with the beasts of the earth.

8/25/11

YOU MUST NOW CONSTANTLY SEEK MY FACE

The enemy is now accelerating and increasing his attacks on the people of the earth. Only the most discerning shall not fall prey to his schemes and trickery at this time.

My people, while it is true I have given you power over all the power of the enemy, you are no match for his wit nor his wiles, and you must now constantly seek My face and pray you will not be caught in his snares, if you are to survive. For he sees the signs of the times and has a plan to destroy each one of you.

In coming months much will change in your world. When judgment comes, it is never an easy thing to see. Know that for all those you see taken, more remain yet who can still be saved, and move your focus to that.

You must not focus on destruction when you see it happen, but pray and watch for My soon return and intercede for the lost still among you. By this will you obtain mercy for yourselves, as you pray for others.

What is coming must come and was foretold long ago. Still, it will be difficult to see. Know that I am with you, My children. My love surrounds you at all times, and MY ANGELS WALK AMONG YOU. I have sent them to guide and help you, and to gather in the harvest.

Cry out to Me for your nations. Mercy can still be shown to some who have not yet rendered their hearts to Me.

Fearsome sights are coming in the earth soon, but you must not fear, My children, for then you shall not be able to hear My voice guiding you. Much is changing now and it shall continue changing.

(I have received emails asking for clarification of this part where the Lord said we would not be able to hear His voice. What He means here is that if we get into fear, we will not be able to hear Him. Fear causes you to not be able to hear God speak.)

Everything that can be shaken I shall shake before My final judgments. Whenever you are tempted to fear, run to your prayer closet and seek My face, and I shall surround you with My love, and comfort you there.

Make ready, My children, for I am coming soon.

1 Peter 5:8: Be sober, be vigilant; because your adversary the devil, as a roaring lion, walketh about, seeking whom he may devour:

Mark 13:33: Take ye heed, watch and pray: for ye know not when the time is.

Matt. 28:20: Teaching them to observe all things whatsoever I have commanded you: and, lo, I am with you always, even unto the end of the world. Amen.

8/29/11

MY PEOPLE MUST TAKE CONTROL OF THEIR MOUTHS

This Word came in a time of prayer.

My people must take control of their mouths and refuse to use them for evil purposes; for much evil is coming upon the earth, and those who do not shall perish.

I desire your lips would praise and worship Me, My people, not criticize, condemn, and curse each other. It is not My desire for you to be talebearers causing wounds to others; yet many of My people continue sinning, knowing what My Holy Word says about this.

DO YOU NOT KNOW YOU ARE SOWING BAD SEEDS OF GOSSIP INTO YOUR OWN LIVES, My children? Do you not know this displeases Me greatly, and I shall not overlook your sins? Do you not think I care when you use your tongues to wound My other children? I am not a careless Father who does not see when you do this.

You think your words do not matter to Me, but they matter a great deal. I am not pleased when you ignore My Word in this way.

Prov. 18:21: Death and life are in the power of the tongue: and they that love it shall eat the fruit thereof.

Prov. 21:23: Whoso keepeth his mouth and his tongue keepeth his soul from troubles.

James 3:10: Out of the same mouth proceedeth blessing and cursing. My brethren, these things ought not so to be.

Eph. 4:29: Let no corrupt communication proceed out of your mouth, but that which is good to the use of edifying, that it may minister grace unto the hearers.

Prov. 26:22: The words of a talebearer are as wounds, and they go down into the innermost parts of the belly.

Gal. 6:7: Be not deceived; God is not mocked: for whatsoever a man soweth, that shall he also reap.

9/3/11

I WILL NOT LOOK THE OTHER WAY

Tell My people to position themselves for battle. Tell them to get ready to fight the enemy of their souls like never before, to fight for purity in their hearts that I may exalt them higher and use them in a greater way.

Tell them to purify their lives of the idols they place before My Holy Name. I will not look the other way as you worship other gods, My children. Did I not say you shall have no other gods before Me? And so it must be.

For I am a jealous God. I love you exceedingly. I must be first in your hearts and minds.

Exodus 20:3: Thou shalt have no other gods before me.

Prov. 20:9: Who can say, I have made my heart clean, I am pure from my sin?

Psalm 51:10: Create in me a clean heart, O God; and renew a right spirit within me.

Exodus 34:14: For thou shalt worship no other god: for the LORD, whose name is Jealous, is a jealous God:

9/09/11

THE TIME OF MY JUDGMENTS HAS COME

I was overcome with grief while looking at a picture of damage from wildfires in Bastrop County, Texas, when the Lord began to speak to me.

What you are feeling is grief over all of My judgments that are now coming in the earth, My daughter, not grief over just one. The time of My judgments has come, and they will be very terrible to see and hear about.

When the Lord spoke this to me, I saw in the Spirit that the judgments will seem to be happening all around the world, and it will be coming from many disasters and events and happenings that are all taking place at almost the same time. When I looked, it seemed as if there was no nation that was not suffering in some way.

My people do not see, and refuse to hear what is coming, but it is coming nevertheless. Those in tune with My Spirit feel what is coming and grieve for the many souls that will be lost in that time. In that time you will also grieve for sin, AS IT IS SIN THAT HAS BROUGHT MY JUDGMENTS UPON YOU.

Cry out, My children, when you feel the pain of a lost and dying world. Cry out to Me to be saved, for the lost to be saved, to be spared from what is soon to come, for there shall be no place to hide in the end. For I am a righteous judge, and I am coming to judge all nations, all peoples. The earth is Mine and the fullness thereof, but now the earth is filled with sin and it must be removed.

Psalm 24:1: The earth is the LORD's, and the fullness thereof; the world, and they that dwell therein.

Psalm 96:13: Before the LORD: for he cometh, for he cometh to judge the earth: he shall judge the world with righteousness, and the people with his truth.

10/01/11

THIS SHALL BE A YEAR OF TURNING

The Lord had been silent for a couple of weeks, and I was making coffee one day when He began to speak this Word to me for Rosh Hashanah, the Jewish New Year.

This year will be a year of great change for My people. I am calling you out. My people have remained hidden, but no more. I am calling you to witness for Me, to repent on behalf of your cities, your nations, to cry out to Me for mercy; for My judgments are falling, and you will see them increase this year. Nations that have turned from Me shall suffer great loss. Nations that refuse to know Me, greater still.

This shall be a year of turning.

In my spirit I saw a sifting taking place. Everything that was sifted went either left or right. In the Spirit I knew every person would either get better—closer to the Lord, or worse—more in the world, because of great adversity that is coming.

My people will either turn to Me or from Me as adversity increases in the earth.

SOME OF YOU ARE READY FOR WHAT IS COMING; MOST ARE NOT. Readiness in your spirits consists of coming before Me daily in repentance, seeking My face, seeking My will in all things, abiding in Me.

Most of you abide in the world and visit Me. I desire you do the reverse. In what is coming, the world cannot save you. It has become a snare to you, My people, for you do not see through its embellishments to the one who tempts you with worldly things.

(As I was thinking about what a strange word "embellishments" was for the Lord to use, He reminded me of a vision He had given me back in about 2000 that I call the Conveyer Belt Vision.

He showed me that people were driving to what they thought would make them happy; and He showed me how actually Satan was behind it, and in reality destruction awaited them at the end of a conveyor belt their car was being moved along on.)

(Later, I looked up embellish in the dictionary and found it made perfect sense. This is what it said: "to decorate or adorn; to improve by adding details. OFTEN FICTITIOUS.")

In this coming year, many who are prepared will be placed on the forefront. (I knew He meant into ministries when He said this, and I thought of that Scripture verse about not putting a lighted candle under a bushel where it is hidden.)

These are those who have submitted to My preparation and refinement for years and have passed the test and been found faithful. I shall now greatly reward you for your efforts to be and stay in My will for your lives.

For those who have refused, there will be further testing. Some of you will suffer greatly because you did not obey Me when you knew I was calling you. (I sensed the Lord's anger here.) *You thought to yourselves, "Let someone else do it," and so your brothers and sisters have a heavier load. You expect Me to bless* you in spite of your disobedience, but you shall now pay the price.

Everything you have, I have given you, yet you refuse Me:

If you have your health, it is by My decree.
If you are prospering, I have ordained it.
If your family is well, I have blessed them.

Yet you take your ease and leave the load for someone else to carry. THIS YEAR YOU SHALL FEEL MY HAND OF JUDGMENT UPON YOU FOR YOUR DISOBEDIENCE. My blessings shall no longer rest on those who refuse to share the load.

For those of you who have given, I have seen your every sacrifice, and you will now start to see tangible rewards for your obedience to Me. As you see others decrease in adversity, I will spare you and I will bless you; and I shall increase you miraculously. And you shall marvel and praise My Holy Name even more. And you shall know that My hand of blessing is truly upon you. Many of you have refused to stop giving even when you yourself were in need. You will receive the greatest blessings of all—you shall know My glory.

Eye has not seen nor ear heard the blessings I have in store for My people in this time. Yes, there will be disasters. Yes, there will be hardship, but My glory shall outshine it all. (At this point I saw in the Spirit a group of many people covered in what appeared to be a wall or a wing of feathers.)

My children, you do not know the greatness of the hour in which you live. Your minds cannot comprehend all that is about to happen in the earth and in the heavenlies. Keep My Word and My Son's name ever before you in this time. It shall lead you and guide you into all you need to know. There is much more coming *in the world than My children realize, but when you abide in Me, you are always prepared, for I Myself shall cause you to be ready. I Myself shall bring you all you need. There is no need for fear of what is to come.*

Keep your eyes on Me. Do you think I will not care for My own? Do you think if you give to My work, I will let you be without? If you are about your Father's business, do you think I will leave you in lack? No, My children, for I am faithful to watch over My Word and perform it at all times. Indeed as you sow into My Kingdom, I shall sow back into your lives all you can ever need and more.

Be found in Me as My judgments fall. Be found obeying Me in all things and walking in My ways. Do not be found in the world, but in Me. Abide in My Word and obey it, and you shall not be in the world.

Separate yourselves to what I have called you to do, and seek My face daily. Repent daily for your sins. Seek to please Me in all things. Do not follow the ways of the world but be found in My ways.

Luke 11:33: No man, when he hath lighted a candle, putteth it in a secret place, neither under a bushel, but on a candlestick, that they which come in may see the light.

John 15:5-6: I am the vine, ye are the branches: He that abideth in me, and I in him, the same bringeth forth much fruit: for without me ye can do nothing. If a man abide not in me, he is cast forth as a branch, and is withered; and men gather them, and cast them into the fire, and they are burned.

1 John 2:15-17: Love not the world, neither the things that are in the world. If any man love the world, the love of the Father is not in him. For all that is in the world, the lust of the flesh, and the lust of the eyes, and the pride of life, is not of the Father, but is of the world. And the world passeth away, and the lust thereof: but he that doeth the will of God abideth for ever.

1 Cor. 2:9: But as it is written, Eye hath not seen, nor ear heard, neither have entered into the heart of man, the things which God hath prepared for them that love him.

Matt. 6:27-29: Which of you by taking thought can add one cubit unto his stature? And why take ye thought for raiment? Consider the lilies of the field, how they grow; they toil not, neither do they spin: And yet I say unto you, That even Solomon in all his glory was not arrayed like one of these.

Psalm 9:17: The wicked shall be turned into hell, and all the nations that forget God.

10/02/11

SO WILL IT BE FOR EVERY NATION THAT FORGETS ME

A heavy sadness rose up in my spirit as I was looking at some family photos from happier times long ago, and I began to pray and ask the Lord what it meant.

The happy days of America will become bygones, never to return again. So will it be for every nation that forgets Me and turns from My righteous ways to their own ways and to wickedness.

Rise up, My people. Rise up to your places in this world, for the battle is beginning, and it rages all around you in the spiritual realm already. You cannot see those who fight for you to keep you safe, who fight for Me and My Kingdom.

The enemy of your souls lurks in the darkness, in crevices and cracks in your lives—places where you have not yet allowed Me to shine My light and cleanse you. These will be the cracks he slips through to destroy you in months to come, if you do not lay down your sins and turn to Me with repentant hearts. Partial repentance is not enough—I require an upright heart of you, not a heart of wicked schemes. You cannot serve Me and the enemy of your souls. You must choose. The time quickly approaches when there will be no more time to choose; YOU MUST CHOOSE NOW, IF YOU ARE TO BE SAFE.

Plans are being made behind the scenes that will lead to destruction. Many lives shall be lost. The enemy seeks to sift you, and he shall be allowed to sift some of you that you may come up higher with Me. He will be allowed to attack many of you because you will read this and refuse still to give up your sinful ways. You justify your sin in your minds and think it does not matter, but truly I tell you, you shall answer to Me for every sin of which you do not honestly repent before Me.

In the times that are coming, there will be no room for sin in your lives. How can you serve two masters who are at war with each other? You must choose one side or the other, or be killed in the crossfire.

Psalm 9:17: The wicked shall be turned into hell, and all the nations that forget God.

1 Peter 5:8: Be sober, be vigilant; because your adversary the devil, as a roaring lion, walketh about, seeking whom he may devour.

Acts 3:19: Repent ye therefore, and be converted, that your sins may be blotted out, when the times of refreshing shall come from the presence of the Lord.

10/09/11

WHY IS YOUR FAITH SO SMALL?

I was praying about the coming judgments and about whether I
needed to do anything more to prepare for them when the Lord
began to speak this Word to me:

*THEM THAT KNOW ME SHALL NOT LACK EVEN IN THE MIDST OF
COMPLETE DISASTER. I shall provide for you all miraculously. You
and many of My children underestimate the lengths I will go to,
to take care of you during this time. You all feel you must
provide for yourselves.*

*How far would you go to feed one of your children and provide
shelter for them and take care of their needs? Do you really
think I would do less?*

*Did I not provide My only begotten Son to provide a way to
Heaven for you? Why is your faith so small after all the miracles
you have seen Me perform?*

Psalm 91:1: He that dwelleth in the secret place of the Most High shall abide
under the shadow of the Almighty. 2. I will say of the LORD, He is my refuge and
my fortress: my God; in him will I trust. 3. Surely he shall deliver thee from the
snare of the fowler, and from the noisome pestilence. 4. He shall cover thee with
his feathers, and under his wings shalt thou trust: his truth shall be thy shield and
buckler. 5. Thou shalt not be afraid for the terror by night; nor for the arrow that
flieth by day; 6. Nor for the pestilence that walketh in darkness; nor for the
destruction that wasteth at noonday. 7. A thousand shall fall at thy side, and ten
thousand at thy right hand; but it shall not come nigh thee. 8. Only with thine eyes
shalt thou behold and see the reward of the wicked. 9. Because thou hast made the
LORD, which is my refuge, even the most High, thy habitation; 10. There shall no
evil befall thee, neither shall any plague come nigh thy dwelling. 11. For he shall
give his angels charge over thee, to keep thee in all thy ways. 12. They shall bear
thee up in their hands, lest thou dash thy foot against a stone. 13. Thou shalt tread
upon the lion and adder: the young lion and the dragon shalt thou trample under
feet. 14. Because he hath set his love upon me, therefore will I deliver him: I will

set him on high, because he hath known my name. 15. He shall call upon me, and I will answer him: I will be with him in trouble; I will deliver him, and honour him. 16. With long life will I satisfy him, and shew him my salvation.

John 3:16: For God so loved the world, that he gave his only begotten Son, that whosoever believeth in him should not perish, but have everlasting life.

10/21/11

ONLY ONE

The days ahead will require you to determine and decide who and what is really your god. Many of you think you know already, but you have never truly been made to choose only one. You think you will choose Me above all others, but you see not the other gods lurking within your mind and heart—gods the enemy used to tempt you away from Me.

At this point I heard heartbreaking sadness in the voice of the Lord, like you would hear in the voice of someone who just found out their spouse was unfaithful.

Some of you have allowed these gods to invade your lives. You have welcomed them. Some of you are even aware of their presence, yet you do nothing to cleanse your hearts of them, thinking I will understand and excuse your sin of idolatry. Did I not say in My Word thou shalt have no other gods before Me? (At this point I heard serious anger in the Lord's voice.) *And so you shall not. If you are Mine, act like it.*

Days coming will bring hard circumstances that will require you to choose which god you will serve. Only one. Think hard and decide well, My children, FOR THIS CHOICE CANNOT BE UNDONE.

Some of My children have already chosen. They have followed Me wherever I led them, laying aside their own dreams and desires and taking up My cross. For them this choice has already been made, and the days to come will be far easier than for others.

For those who have remained enmeshed in the world and all of its temptations, the times to come will be very hard indeed; for you have lived a soft life, putting your faith in what you can see instead of in Me. Your faith is flimsy. It is like a reed that bends with every new wind of doctrine. You are easily deceived because you have not built your house of faith on the rock of My Son.

You must choose which god you will serve for the rest of your earthly lives. That is the god you will serve in eternity as well.

My children, many of you underestimate the importance and lateness of the time you live in. You do not see My Son's return approaching. Did I not say "like a thief in the night?" Yet many of you do nothing to prepare yourselves for His soon return.

Will His bride not ready herself for her Groom? Will you be found not dressed when the wedding party arrives? Will you be left behind?

You must think on these things now while there is still time, and choose well. In the days soon coming, chaos shall abound in many nations. There will be very little time to think later for some of you who read this Word. YOUR LIVES WILL BE CUT SHORT BECAUSE OF THIS DISASTER OR THAT UPRISING.

Do not make the mistake of thinking you have more time than you do. Some decisions should not be put off until another time. Do not be like the rich man in My Word who stored up in his barns and set himself to enjoy his worldly pleasures, whose soul was required of him that night; for you know not the seriousness of all that is about to transpire.

Do not wait. Choose now. Which god will you serve?

I have given you all you need to survive and prosper in this time. You need only ask to receive of what I have for you.

Adversity has risen up against you time and time again. Many of you have prayed and asked why this is so. Adversity is your teacher, My children. ADVERSITY BRINGS HARDSHIP THAT PREPARES YOU FOR WHAT IS HARDER STILL, that is yet to come.

Trust Me. I can see further down the road into your future, you cannot. This is why you must allow Me to guide your paths and not try to understand every tiny nuance of what happens. It is not always for you to understand, but for you to simply obey Me in faith, trusting that I love you. I know what is best for all concerned.

This next year shall bring many changes you cannot see from where you are. I AM TRYING TO POSITION EACH OF YOU TO BE READY FOR THESE CHANGES BUT SOME OF YOU RESIST MY PATHS. This will cause further hardship to come into your lives. OFTEN WHAT MY CHILDREN SUFFER IS A RESULT OF NOT OBEYING ME AT SOME EARLIER TIME.

Some of what is to come is far worse than My children are expecting. I am trying to protect you by guiding your paths to a safer place. Obey Me and all shall be well. Resist and you are left with the results of your own way.

Come up higher with Me. Let us commune together as you worship Me in Spirit and in truth. Allow Me to prepare you for all that is to come.

Matthew 6:24: No man can serve two masters: for either he will hate the one, and love the other; or else he will hold to the one, and despise the other. Ye cannot serve God and mammon.

Exodus 20:3: Thou shalt have no other gods before me.

Matthew 11:7: And as they departed, Jesus began to say unto the multitudes concerning John, What went ye out into the wilderness to see? A reed shaken with the wind?

James 4:4: Ye adulterers and adulteresses, know ye not that the friendship of the world is enmity with God? whosoever therefore will be a friend of the world is the enemy of God.

1 Peter 2:7-8: Unto you therefore which believe he is precious: but unto them which be disobedient, the stone which the builders disallowed, the same is made the head of the corner, And a stone of stumbling, and a rock of offence, even to them which stumble at the Word, being disobedient: whereunto also they were appointed.

Luke 12:16-20: And he spake a parable unto them, saying, The ground of a certain rich man brought forth plentifully: And he thought within himself, saying, What shall I do, because I have no room where to bestow my fruits? And he said, This will I do: I will pull down my barns, and build greater; and there will I bestow all my fruits and my goods. And I will say to my soul, Soul, thou hast much goods laid up for many years; take thine ease, eat, drink, and be merry. But God said unto him, Thou fool, this night thy soul shall be required of thee: then whose shall those things be, which thou hast provided?

Joshua 24:15: And if it seem evil unto you to serve the LORD, choose you this day whom ye will serve; whether the gods which your fathers served that were on the other side of the flood, or the gods of the Amorites, in whose land ye dwell: but as for me and my house, we will serve the LORD.

Isaiah 30:20: And though the Lord give you the bread of adversity, and the water of affliction, yet shall not thy teachers be removed into a corner any more, but thine eyes shall see thy teachers:

Proverbs 3:5-7: Trust in the LORD with all thine heart; and lean not unto thine own understanding. In all thy ways acknowledge him, and he shall direct thy paths. Be not wise in thine own eyes: fear the LORD, and depart from evil.

John 4:23: But the hour cometh, and now is, when the true worshippers shall worship the Father in Spirit and in truth: for the Father seeketh such to worship him.

10/27/11

BE VIGILANT

My people have become slack while waiting for My words to come to pass. They mistakenly think they have more time than they do. I desire they would stay vigilant and remain watchful, for the enemy often lulls them to sleep in this way.

My Kingdom does not operate on your system of time, My people. Once I have spoken something, it is sure to come to pass, for it is ordained by Me. I created all things, and I created time as well, that you may measure it. However in eternity there is no time.

Things are coming soon in the earth you will not understand. The enemy moves quickly against My people in the earth, and he has made many plans of destruction. Some of his plans will fail, but others shall succeed. It is necessary that each of you listen for My leading,

AND PAY HEED TO THE LEADINGS INSIDE YOUR SPIRIT THAT COME FROM ME, FOR I SHALL LEAD YOU TO SAFETY IN THIS WAY FROM EVENTS THAT ARE PLANNED AGAINST YOU.

Days grow darker and darker in the earth, and evil abounds on every side. My Word has foretold these things and much more, but there is even more yet to come that you know not of. Be vigilant against the enemy of your souls. Be found watching and praying at all times, for danger lurks in places you cannot see. I will protect you if you obey Me in all things.

There is much work to be done to bring the harvest of souls into My Kingdom. I desire My people would spend time each day interceding for lost souls, that more may be saved from eternal damnation. My people are about too many things that have no eternal value; they are still playing in the world.

Do you not know the lateness of the hour, My children? Do you not realize you will answer to Me for how you spend your time now? Do you not desire that your heavenly reward would be great? Or has the enemy lulled you to sleep while you waited on My words to come to pass in your life?

Many of you have suffered long and laborious trials, trials where you lost many of your earthly possessions. You cried out to Me and asked why. Many of you suffer still in your walk with Me, fighting to hang on to your faith. I say to you now that your faith shall be greatly rewarded. Your perseverance shall be greatly rewarded. There is nothing you do for My Name's sake that I do not notice. There is nothing you do for Me that you will not be rewarded for and greatly so.

For some of you I shall reveal to you the reasons for your long trials in days to come. Others will know later. SOME OF YOU, HOWEVER, HAVE BROUGHT YOUR TRIALS UPON YOURSELVES WHEN YOU DID NOT HEED MY VOICE OF WARNING TO YOU AT AN EARLIER TIME. Often I am blamed for trials My children suffer which they brought upon themselves by sin, ignoring My warnings, or other disobedience. This should not be so, My children, for I am a loving and a faithful Father. How can I keep you safe if you will not obey Me?

How will you survive what is coming when you continue to go your own way?

Mark 13:33: Take ye heed, watch and pray: for ye know not when the time is.

Isaiah 60:2: For, behold, the darkness shall cover the earth, and gross darkness the people: but the LORD shall arise upon thee, and his glory shall be seen upon thee.

1 Peter 5:8: Be sober, be vigilant; because your adversary the devil, as a roaring lion, walketh about, seeking whom he may devour:

Ephesians 6:12: For we wrestle not against flesh and blood, but against principalities, against powers, against the rulers of the darkness of this world, against spiritual wickedness in high places.

Matthew 12:36: But I say unto you, That every idle word that men shall speak, they shall give account thereof in the day of judgment.

11/05/11

THE DAYS GROW DARKER STILL

I was praying about a message for a Thursday night's Blog Talk Radio Show when the Lord began to speak this to me:

Tell My children they must prepare for the coming year in a special way, a way unfamiliar to many of them. This next year will bring challenges many have not faced before, challenges you will be unfamiliar with. The challenges in each country will vary. Many of you will be moving into a new spiritual level this next year, a new level in Me.

THIS SHALL BE A NEW LEVEL OF MY MIRACULOUS PROVISION, something few of you are accustomed to.

It is imperative you remain calm as the changes take place in your lives that will take you to this new level. The enemy will do his best to get you to fear, but I desire you fear not. I desire your complete trust and obedience. Those who will not obey Me and those who refuse to trust Me will find their paths difficult in coming months.

SOME I AM MOVING INTO THE TIME OF THE FULFILLMENT OF YOUR DREAMS AND DESIRES I Myself have placed in your hearts for just such a time as this. You have been refined and prepared that you may arise and shine in this hour.

Many of you who have veered from the path of what is right missed My original plan, but I have another plan you will fulfill. Yes, there is still much work, My children, before the harvest, and all have tasks to perform.

How much you have allowed Me to refine you determines how greatly you can be used in this time. If you have rejected knowledge, if you have rejected wisdom, if you refuse still to walk in My ways, what use shall you serve in the harvest of souls?

The new year upcoming shall bring shocking events, events you have not seen before. It shall be a year of firsts in so many ways. My true children shall remain unafraid, no matter what they see happen in the world.

The world about you is full of unrest, My children, and it groans for the return of My Son. More and increasing unrest is coming. It is a time when you will increasingly rely on My peace to sustain you, for nothing about you shall seem certain; and truly much is not what it appears to be.

Walk closer to Me still than ever before, and I shall lead you in the way that you should go. There is a way that seems right in a man's own heart, but you need My wisdom to survive this.

The way shall be dark before you as the days grow darker still. There is little light in the earth now and few who walk in My ways. I shall guide and protect My own; I shall light your way. Walk close to Me each day. I will cause your path to shine before you

Isaiah 41:10: Fear thou not; for I am with thee: be not dismayed; for I am thy God: I will strengthen thee; yea, I will help thee; yea, I will uphold thee with the right hand of my righteousness.

Hosea 4:6: My people are destroyed for lack of knowledge: because thou hast rejected knowledge, I will also reject thee, that thou shalt be no priest to me: seeing thou hast forgotten the law of thy God, I will also forget thy children.

Isaiah 48:10: Behold, I have refined thee, but not with silver; I have chosen thee in the furnace of affliction.

Isaiah 26:3: Thou wilt keep him in perfect peace, whose mind is stayed on thee: because he trusteth in thee.

Proverbs 14:12: There is a way which seemeth right unto a man, but the end thereof are the ways of death.

Psalm 119:105: Thy Word is a lamp unto my feet, and a light unto my path.

Proverbs 4:18: But the path of the just is as the shining light, that shineth more and more unto the perfect day.

11/10/11

CHANGE IS COMING

I had a really restless evening yesterday and woke up in the wee hours of the morning and could not go back to sleep, even after praying. I found out today that many others also felt it, so I began to seek the Lord about what we were sensing. This is what He said:

This land has known a time of ease and prosperity, and prosperity made fools of many who found the world too alluring to resist. I shall begin to tear down the false gods My people have chosen over Me and reveal their powerlessness one by one.

Some of you will weep as you see your false gods destroyed, but this must be done, that you may know Me as the one true living

God. Your false gods are only illusions the enemy has devised to steal your worship away from Me.

Many of you have felt a stirring in the Spirit of late. You have felt weeping in your soul for the lost, those who do not know Me. You have felt My grief at those who will be lost in the end.

The time has come for My judgments to be rendered in the earth. Many lives shall be lost in what is coming. Many souls will be lost to the enemy if My people do not obey Me in this time. I desire My people would pray focused prayers—for the lost, for their cities, for their nations—that I may show mercy. IF MY PEOPLE DO NOT OBEY ME, SOME OF THE LOST WILL BE AMONG THEIR OWN FAMILIES AND LOVED ONES. They shall suffer greatly for their lack of obedience in this time.

Tell them. Tell them I am coming. Tell them to be ready to hear My commands. Tell them to start praying and not cease until it is over. Tell them I am coming.

You shall see fearful sights. Men's hearts truly will fail them in what they see. A change is coming. Things will not ever go back the way they were, after this change. This change will not appear the way you think it will. It will come softly, but it is a big change, behind the scenes, and the impact will be high. The change will not be evident immediately, but over time. Once it has taken place, however, it will not revert. You will not be able to miss this change once it has taken place, and you will know what it is.

You must tell My people how to prepare for this change. Tell them I love them. (I heard such incredible sadness and grief in His voice when He said that He loves us!)

Tell them My judgments are righteous, and those who are judged now have time to repent. (There are people in whose lives God's hand of judgment is already beginning to fall. I saw in my spirit that these were the ones He meant here.)

Those who are judged later will not.

Tell My people to pass before Me and repent of every sin they know of they have, and let Me help them. (I saw His throne in my spirit, and felt He meant to pass before His throne by praying.) *The time to turn from your sins is now—do not wait, My children! Do not wait, for time is much shorter than you think. Come before Me and confess your sins now, for My judgments are coming to your land, and many of you will not have time later.* (I felt a really terrible heaviness in my spirit when He said that.) *You must not neglect to do this. Even sins you think of as small must be confessed that I may forgive you now, and you must turn from them. What is coming in this next year will create a rocky path for many of you to walk on; your times will not be easy.*

Difficulties shall abound all around you.

The changes you see happening now are only the very beginning. Some of you believe everything will return as it was and that it will be "business as usual," but it shall not be so. Change is here to stay.

In coming months, you shall feel as if you are standing on shifting sands, for there will be constant change. Some of these changes you may suspect are coming; others will be complete surprises to many of you.

It is time to move forward, My people, for time is short.

Psalm 96:5: For all the gods of the nations are idols: but the LORD made the heavens.

Psalm 106:36: And they served their idols: which were a snare unto them.

Luke 21:25-26: And there shall be signs in the sun, and in the moon, and in the stars; and upon the earth distress of nations, with perplexity; the sea and the waves roaring; Men's hearts failing them for fear, and for looking after those things which are coming on the earth: for the powers of heaven shall be shaken.

Joel 2:13: And rend your heart, and not your garments, and turn unto the LORD your God: for he is gracious and merciful, slow to anger, and of great kindness, and repenteth him of the evil.

11/17/11

GREAT CHANGES

I was thinking about a close friend who was going through a divorce and how she has adapted to all the changes the divorce has brought into her life, when the Lord began to speak this Word to me today:

In this New Year, as change rolls out across the earth, many will find they can no longer live their old ways. Change will be required in order to survive. My people will be led to change beforehand.

My people shall rise up to this change as if they expected it, for I will prepare them beforehand for what is coming. Those near Me who walk in My ways will be prepared. Much change is indeed coming, great changes you know not of.

It is of utmost importance My people walk in complete obedience to Me at this time. There is no time for dragging your feet—for resisting change when I bring it into your lives. I am preparing you for what lies ahead, My people, and if you resist, you will not be ready when change is forced upon you. Yield to My gentle leading.

A time of much chaos is approaching in the world. Stable systems are no longer stable; leaders no longer lead and guide, but fall themselves into traps the enemy has set for them. Some of these I give way to fall; others are tempted and give in to what they know they should not do. They will be found out. The time when systems in place operated faithfully is gone now to make way for change.

Change is coming, and those who deny it are deceived. Those who resist it will be taken forcefully by it and will not be ready. THOSE WHO YIELD TO ME AND MY LEADING WILL BE HIDDEN IN ME AS THE CHANGES COME. Ready and prepared, they will not be devastated by events soon to happen.

The stage has been set and now is ready for all My Word has foretold. The Man of Perdition shall soon appear. He comes to deceive and destroy all mankind. He shall have his way with many. There are many in the world who are willing to be deceived for wealth, for pleasure, or for the sake of being exalted among men.

THEY DO NOT BELIEVE IN WHAT IS YET TO COME BUT CONSIDER IT A FAIRY TALE OF SORTS DEVISED BY THE WEAK. They shall know they have been deceived in the end.

My children, stay close to Me, for what is coming in the world shall indeed terrify many. It is not My will that you would be afraid, for these things must happen.

Thessalonians 2:1-4: Now we beseech you, brethren, by the coming of our Lord Jesus Christ, and by our gathering together unto him, That ye be not soon shaken in mind, or be troubled, neither by spirit, nor by word, nor by letter as from us, as that the day of Christ is at hand. Let no man deceive you by any means: for that day shall not come, except there come a falling away first, and that man of sin be revealed, the son of perdition; Who opposeth and exalteth himself above all that is called God, or that is worshipped; so that he as God sitteth in the temple of God, showing himself that he is God.

11/24/11

IT IS TIME

It is time for My children to take up their crosses. Many of My children have been lax to truly lay down the pleasures of their flesh. You think you can take your pleasures into the future in what I have called you to do. You cannot.

(When He spoke this last part, I heard in the Spirit a ripping or tearing sound.)

Time will make you choose. You cannot walk a steep hill carrying your much baggage. You must choose what you will lay down for Me, for My Name's sake, or you must stay behind the others.

What will you choose?

It is time My children stopped their attacks on one another. You think you judge in My Name and attack, but you do not. Did My Son judge in harshness or in love? Did He attack those who were seeking Me? Nay, He did not. He loved all who came seeking My Kingdom, and so should you also; but many of you devise your own standards for how My children should behave, and you attack them when they do not. It is time to stop your attacks on My children and walk in love. Did I not say love your neighbor as yourself? Yet you show yourself much mercy, and show your neighbor none! It is an unjust balance, which is an abomination in My sight.

I love you all with a love that knows no bounds, but My Name is righteousness and truth, justice, mercy, and honor. My children shall walk in these as well—if they are to be called My own.

These are perilous times, My children. The times you walk in are like none that have come before, and soon you shall know it.

Players shall appear on the world stage unlike any you have encountered before now. Events shall come which will cause you to reel in shock. Yet you know these things must happen, as My Word foretells, and will soon be.

You have decisions to make. Will you serve Me? Will you serve Me to the end, no matter the cost? Or will you continue to serve your flesh?

Matthew 10:38: And he that taketh not his cross, and followeth after me, is not worthy of me.

Matthew 16:24: Then said Jesus unto his disciples, If any man will come after me, let him deny himself, and take up his cross, and follow me.

Luke 9:23: And he said to them all, If any man will come after me, let him deny himself, and take up his cross daily, and follow me.

Deut. 25:14-16: Thou shalt not have in thine house divers measures, a great and a small. But thou shalt have a perfect and just weight, a perfect and just measure shalt thou have: that thy days may be lengthened in the land which the LORD thy God giveth thee. For all that do such things, and all that do unrighteously, are an abomination unto the LORD thy God.

Proverbs 20:23: Divers weights are an abomination unto the LORD; and a false balance is not good.

Luke 10:27: And he answering said, Thou shalt love the Lord thy God with all thy heart, and with all thy soul, and with all thy strength, and with all thy mind; and thy neighbour as thyself.

Gal. 5:14: For all the law is fulfilled in one word, even in this; Thou shalt love thy neighbour as thyself.

Micah 6:8: He hath showed thee, O man, what is good; and what doth the LORD require of thee, but to do justly, and to love mercy, and to walk humbly with thy God?

John 13:35: By this shall all men know that ye are my disciples, if ye have love one to another.

2 Timothy 3:1: This know also, that in the last days perilous times shall come.

Matthew 24:13: But he that shall endure unto the end, the same shall be saved.

Galatians 6:8: For he that soweth to his flesh shall of the flesh reap corruption; but he that soweth to the Spirit shall of the Spirit reap life everlasting.

11/28/11

THEY SHALL BE DECEIVED

I was in my prayer time and near the end of it, when the Lord began giving me things to pray for that He has never led me to pray about before. *He led me to pray over the safety of the food I eat today, my internet connection, my electricity, water supply, and the air I breathe.* This was something new, and after I prayed it, I sat quietly before Him, and He began to speak this Word:

My children, a dangerous time approaches. Dangers now lurk where none did before, and you must be diligent in prayer—for yourselves and also for those you love. Many in the world seek to harm My people. Many would see you destroyed— annihilated!

There is coming one who desires this much more than those before him, and he will strive against all that is of Me and My Kingdom purposes. WATCH FOR HIM TO APPEAR. Know that his intent is evil only. He does not bring peace, though he claims to. HIS PEACE TALK OPENS THE DOORS FOR HIM TO CAUSE MY PEOPLE HARM, to bring war.

It is this one who will cause My people to rise and fight against each other as never before. Brother against brother. Did I not say in My Word these days would come? And so shall it be.

Strive to walk in love one with another, for in love are you protected from sin. Those who fail to walk in love shall fall quickly to the enemy's plan in these last days, for they shall be deceived and their hearts darkened.

My children, I have long been preparing you for this time. Rise up in My strength and declare My Word boldly. Pray for the lost and for your loved ones. Pray to be counted worthy, and stand. STAND; DO NOT FALL AWAY THOUGH THE TEMPTATION BE GREAT. Stand in the truth of My words.

Matthew 10:21: And the brother shall deliver up the brother to death, and the father the child: and the children shall rise up against their parents, and cause them to be put to death.

John 13:34-35: A new commandment I give unto you, That ye love one another; as I have loved you, that ye also love one another. By this shall all men know that ye are my disciples, if ye have love one to another.

Ephesians 5:2: And walk in love, as Christ also hath loved us, and hath given himself for us an offering and a sacrifice to God for a sweet smelling savour.

12/1/11

RESPONSE TO INQUIRIES ABOUT ATTACKS

I was praying and inquiring of the Lord about the many emails and phone calls I received this past week about Christians attacking other Christians. I myself have also come under attack in the last week. This is what the Lord said about the attacks.

The greatest attacks are yet to come, My children. You see an increase in the attacks of others upon you even now, but I tell you that far greater attacks than these are coming, and many of you shall not endure. BY THIS METHOD DOES THE ENEMY CAUSE MANY TO FALL, TO STUMBLE, AND TO LOSE THEIR HOLD ON SALVATION. THEY SIMPLY STOP BELIEVING IN ME because their eyes are distracted to those around them.

My people, you are called to believe in Me and stand on My Word alone, but you judge Me by what you see in those in the earth who are only human vessels of My nature. Why do you not seek Me and know Me for yourselves? Why do you insist that I am like them when I have called you all to be like Me?

In times coming, above all else, I desire that you would love one another.

Matthew 18:7: Woe unto the world because of offences! for it must needs be that offences come; but woe to that man by whom the offence cometh!

Philippians 1:9-11: And this I pray, that your love may abound yet more and more in knowledge and in all judgment; That ye may approve things that are excellent; that ye may be sincere and without offence till the day of Christ. Being filled with the fruits of righteousness, which are by Jesus Christ, unto the glory and praise of God.

John 13:35: By this shall all men know that ye are my disciples, if ye have love one to another.

Romans 12:10: Be kindly affectioned one to another with brotherly love; in honour preferring one another;

12/09/11

A SAD TIME IS APPROACHING

My people, a sad time is approaching for the nation of America, for her sins have come up before Me. Long have I pleaded with you to repent, but you would not, and now the once great nation of America, founded on My Name, must be judged.

MANY WHO CALL THEMSELVES BY MY NAME ARE NOT MINE.

Indeed there is nothing in their lives that even looks like Me. Did I not say in My Holy Word, do not take My Name in vain? Why have you called yourself Mine when you belong to the world you live in?

Do you believe your superficial belief in Me can stand before My judgment? Do you speak truth when you say you know Me? HOW CAN YOU KNOW ME WHEN YOU NEVER MAKE TIME FOR ME?

What is coming in the earth is truly too evil for your minds to comprehend; YET MANY OF MY PEOPLE STILL DO NOT BELIEVE MY JUDGMENTS ARE NEAR AND SHALL BE CAUGHT UNPREPARED.

When I strike America, all the nations of the earth shall be affected. Her misery shall echo around the world.

Exodus 20:7: Thou shalt not take the name of the LORD thy God in vain; for the LORD will not hold him guiltless that taketh his name in vain.

Rev. 3:15-17: I know thy works, that thou art neither cold nor hot: I would thou wert cold or hot. So then because thou art lukewarm, and neither cold nor hot, I will spue thee out of my mouth. Because thou sayest, I am rich, and increased with goods, and have need of nothing; and knowest not that thou art wretched, and miserable, and poor, and blind, and naked:

1 John 2:15-16: Love not the world, neither the things that are in the world. If any man love the world, the love of the Father is not in him. For all that is in the world, the lust of the flesh, and the lust of the eyes, and the pride of life, is not of the Father, but is of the world.

Matthew 16:26: For what is a man profited, if he shall gain the whole world, and lose his own soul? or what shall a man give in exchange for his soul?

2 Cor. 5:10: For we must all appear before the judgment seat of Christ; that every one may receive the things done in his body, according to that he hath done, whether it be good or bad.

12/10/11

SHE HAS TURNED AGAINST ME

I was at home tonight, and suddenly a deep sadness filled my spirit. Being unsure of what it meant, I went into prayer and inquired of the Lord about it.

Many changes are coming to the nation of America, and they will not be good ones. As you know, MY HAND OF JUDGMENT IS UPON THIS NATION, and though those in power shall try to fix what is wrong, they shall be unable, for I am behind it. No man and no nation can stand against My mighty power.

Long has this nation's sins come up before Me, and it has become a stench to Me. A nation of people who once proclaimed My Name, that now attempts to cast Me far from its land, but it shall not, for I shall judge all those within its borders who attempt to do so, and you shall see them fall—one by one! What once was Mine can never be truly taken from Me, though it may turn away of its own accord.

Long have My people cried for mercy and for change. Change is coming, My people, THOUGH IT SHALL NOT BE THE CHANGE YOU HAVE DESIRED. The mercies I will pour out upon My own in this time. The lines drawn between My people and those who belong to the world shall be clear for all to see, just as they were in Egypt in the time of Pharaoh.

Once I made America strong against her enemies, but she has turned against Me, the Mighty One of Israel. Now I shall make her enemies strong against her, but My mercy shall rest upon My children.

Exodus 8:21-23: Else, if thou wilt not let my people go, behold, I will send swarms of flies upon thee, and upon thy servants, and upon thy people, and into thy houses: and the houses of the Egyptians shall be full of swarms of flies, and also the ground whereon they are. And I will sever in that day the land of Goshen, in which my people dwell, that no swarms of flies shall be there; to the end thou mayest know that I am the LORD in the midst of the earth. And I will put a division between my people and thy people: tomorrow shall this sign be.

Jeremiah 34:20: I will even give them into the hand of their enemies, and into the hand of them that seek their life: and their dead bodies shall be for meat unto the fowls of the heaven, and to the beasts of the earth.

12/20/11

HIS ATTACKS HAVE INCREASED

Check your foundations, My children, for the enemy of your souls will soon be checking them, searching for a way into your life. He has always done this, but in times to come, in times of distress, in times when you are distracted, cracks appear that are easy access for him.

He seeks to kill, steal, or destroy you; and others he gains access to through you. Be on guard, My children, for his attacks have recently increased and will increase more and more in the coming year.

HE WILL TURN THOSE NEAR YOU AGAINST YOU WHERE HE CAN— pray for them. Pray for them now while there is yet time. He will plunder your houses, attack your health and your finances, but those who are hidden in Me shall not fear.

Those who do My will and walk in My ways shall know My protection.

I love you, My children. The times at hand are perilous, but you have My love and My Word to light the way before you.

John 10:10: The thief cometh not, but for to steal, and to kill, and to destroy: I am come that they might have life, and that they might have it more abundantly.

Psalm 11:2-3: For, lo, the wicked bend their bow, they make ready their arrow upon the string, that they may privily shoot at the upright in heart. If the foundations be destroyed, what can the righteous do?

Luke 6:47-49: Whosoever cometh to me, and heareth my sayings, and doeth them, I will show you to whom he is like: He is like a man which built an house, and digged deep, and laid the foundation on a rock: and when the flood arose, the stream beat vehemently upon that house, and could not shake it: for it was founded upon a rock. But he that heareth, and doeth not, is like a man that without a foundation built an house upon the earth; against which the stream did beat vehemently, and immediately it fell; and the ruin of that house was great.

2 Timothy 3:1: This know also, that in the last days perilous times shall come.

Psalm 119:105: Thy Word is a lamp unto my feet, and a light unto my path.

12/21/11

THE TIME OF SHAKING IS UPON YOU

Many of My children have been feeling a sense of shaking inside. Many have seen visions or dreams of shaking and things being shaken. The shaking is now here and is still coming, My children, for the time of shaking is upon you.

Everything inside man will be shaken to its core. If he is an unbeliever, he will shake with fear. Those who walk in My ways will shake with the anointing of My mighty power on their lives and will go forth in this time and do mighty exploits in My Name!

The world too is being shaken—governments are shaking, economies are shaking, nations stand on the brink quaking, uncertain of what the future holds.

THE FUTURE OF EVERY MAN AND EVERY NATION IS IN MY HAND, and I render judgment according to your deeds. Those who think I do not see their sins are mistaken. Those of you who think I do not care are mistaken. I both care and see—both about you and about your deeds.

MANY IN THE WORLD DO NOT SEE THE TIME ON THE SPIRITUAL CLOCK.

Many do not wish to be distracted from their worldly pleasures and pursuits. They have no time for the God who created them, who ordains their blessings and their next breath of life. They do not see it is My mighty hand that allows them to enjoy the pleasures they do.

Oh man who has no time for Me, the world has become your god, and it shall you serve, though you will long for Me in days to come! You will cry out for Me in your distress and wish to know Me, but circumstances will make it difficult for you to learn of Me in that time.

Why pursue you gods of wood and stone who can neither save nor protect you from what is coming? Why do you worship what you see, which quickly turns to dust and which you cannot carry from this time?

Luke 21:25-26: And there shall be signs in the sun, and in the moon, and in the stars; and upon the earth distress of nations, with perplexity; the sea and the waves roaring; Men's hearts failing them for fear, and for looking after those things which are coming on the earth: for the powers of heaven shall be shaken.

Ezekiel 38:19: For in my jealousy and in the fire of my wrath have I spoken, Surely in that day there shall be a great shaking in the land of Israel;

Romans 2:3: And thinkest thou this, O man, that judgest them which do such things, and doest the same, that thou shalt escape the judgment of God?

Jeremiah 17:10: I the LORD search the heart, I try the reins, even to give every man according to his ways, and according to the fruit of his doings.

Daniel 5:23: But hast lifted up thyself against the Lord of Heaven; and they have brought the vessels of his house before thee, and thou, and thy lords, thy wives, and thy concubines, have drunk wine in them; and thou hast praised the gods of silver, and gold, of brass, iron, wood, and stone, which see not, nor hear, nor know: and the God in whose hand thy breath is, and whose are all thy ways, hast thou not glorified:

12/22/11

THE TIME HAS COME TO PROMOTE MY PEOPLE

I was in my evening prayer time before going to bed, and I began feeling anticipation in my spirit when the Lord began to speak this Word to me:

A time of promotions has come. The time has come to promote My people who have walked in My ways. THOSE WHO HAVE TRULY LAID DOWN ALL TO SERVE ME WILL NOW SEE CLEARLY MY HAND OF BLESSING UPON THEIR LIVES. Those around you shall also see it and know it is My hand.

Much difficulty lies ahead in the coming year, My children. Difficulties of many kinds are approaching, a time like none you have seen before: A time of great difficulty when many shall not know where to turn for help or hope.

You are My voice in the earth, My little ones, and I desire you would speak My love and mercy and hope to those who shall be afflicted in what is soon to come.

Arm yourselves. Arm yourselves with My Word and My wisdom. Know it well, for it shall benefit not only you but all those around you as well. Do not fear what is coming, but stand ready to do all I have called you to do. Know you are My chosen for this time and be glad, My children. Be very glad, for great is your honor in Heaven, and great shall be your reward.

Some of you have felt the changes taking place in the unseen realm. Much is being readied in preparation for the battle soon to come. ANGELIC BEINGS SURROUND MY PEOPLE ON THE EARTH READY TO CARRY OUT MY COMMANDS. The enemy also has forces ready in an attempt to stop the work of My Kingdom, but he shall not succeed. Prepare for battle, My children. Prepare well for the battle soon to come.

I shall raise up some among you to be great leaders in this time. They shall seem to come out of nowhere, for I have kept them hidden for such a time as this. I have prepared them well and made them strong and mighty in battle. They shall not be moved by what they see or what they feel, but only by their Master's voice calling to them.

The year that lies ahead will be difficult for many, but it shall be a joyous one for many of My children who have walked in obedience to Me, for NOW THEY SHALL BEGIN TO SEE THE REWARDS OF THEIR MUCH OBEDIENCE.

Psalm 75:6-7: For promotion cometh neither from the east, nor from the west, nor from the south. But God is the judge: he putteth down one, and setteth up another.

Jude 1:2: Mercy unto you, and peace, and love, be multiplied.

Matthew 20:16: So the last shall be first, and the first last: for many be called, but few chosen.

Zechariah 10:5: And they shall be as mighty men, which tread down their enemies in the mire of the streets in the battle: and they shall fight, because the LORD is with them, and the riders on horses shall be confounded.

12/29/11

WHICH IS MORE IMPORTANT?

Times are coming soon when you will not understand what is happening or why certain things are taking place in the world, My people. Some of you have decided in your minds how the end of days shall play out, but you are mistaken. There are things coming you know not of that will confuse you. No man knows the day or the hour. He also does not know My whole plan, for I did not reveal every detail to you in My Word.

To those who are watching and praying continually for Me, it will not matter. You await My Son's return with great joy, and you have learned to be abased or abound in your present state, and so you are happy either way; and this I desire.

I desire you would be about My work and loving My people each day. I desire you would be increasing the unity among you each day. I desire you would be learning more about My Word and My ways and avoiding the Evil One each day, for these things are more needful than your trying to guess the day of My Son's return. Sufficient for each day is the evil thereof.

Do you not see the lost are dying every day? Do you not know how My heart grieves for them when this happens; and My people are busy talking about My return, when I have pleaded with them to spend time in prayer for the lost?

Which is more important? When I will return or what I will find upon My return?

Luke 21:36: Watch ye therefore, and pray always, that ye may be accounted worthy to escape all these things that shall come to pass, and to stand before the Son of man.

Psalm 133:1: Behold, how good and how pleasant it is for brethren to dwell together in unity!

John 13:34-35: A new commandment I give unto you, That ye love one another; as I have loved you, that ye also love one another. By this shall all men know that ye are my disciples, if ye have love one to another.

Matthew 6:34: Take therefore no thought for the morrow: for the morrow shall take thought for the things of itself. Sufficient unto the day is the evil thereof.

12/29/11

YOU ARE TO BE THAT LIGHT

I was lying down, and just before I went to sleep the Lord began to speak this Word to me:

What makes the night beautiful, daughter?

The lights against it, Lord.

Why is that beautiful?

The contrast, Lord. The dark backdrop makes the light appear that much brighter.

Attention is drawn to that light. It is impossible to stare at the darkness and ignore the beauty of the light which pierces it. Right?

Yes, Lord.

You are to be that light. All My children are to be that light. In days coming, My light shall rest upon you, My children. It shall rest upon you and shine through those of you who have made yourselves ready to do My will.

Now is the time you have been preparing for. The enemy is preparing to release an attack of untold proportions on My people, and parts of his plan will shock you. Those who have not been preparing, who have not spent time in My Word, who are not walking in My ways, shall be caught off guard when this attack is launched. They will not understand how to survive in the time coming. I have left them weapons, but they have not learned to use them.

It is not My desire that you should be caught off guard; yet so many of you take My Words lightly. The enemy has deceived you into thinking there is time without end, and that is a lie. Did I not say in My Word, watch and pray? Yet so many have fallen into a deep, comfortable sleep. The churches have lulled them to sleep, and they know not the enemy is lurking just outside the door, waiting.

Isaiah 60:1-2: Arise, shine; for thy light is come, and the glory of the LORD is risen upon thee. For, behold, the darkness shall cover the earth, and gross darkness the people: but the LORD shall arise upon thee, and his glory shall be seen upon thee.

Matthew 5:14: Ye are the light of the world. A city that is set on an hill cannot be hid.

Matthew 5:16: Let your light so shine before men, that they may see your good works, and glorify your Father which is in heaven.

2 Corinthians 10:4: (For the weapons of our warfare are not carnal, but mighty through God to the pulling down of strong holds;)

Mark 13:33: Take ye heed, watch and pray: for ye know not when the time is.

Ephesians 5:14: Wherefore he saith, Awake thou that sleepest, and arise from the dead, and Christ shall give thee light.

1 Thessalonians 5:6: Therefore let us not sleep, as do others; but let us watch and be sober.

1/01/2012

2012 - MANY CHANGES, MIRACLES

Go forth. Go forth now and preach My gospel, My people. This time is like no other before it. You are living in a time of great changes, of transition.

The enemy of your souls is hard at work trying to defeat you, but many of you have stood strong against him and allowed him not. This year you shall be rewarded for standing.

THIS SHALL BE A YEAR OF MIGHTY MIRACLES AMONG MY PEOPLE.

For My people who are called by My Name shall go forth and do mighty exploits for Me this year. Even those of you who think you have been left behind, who feel unimportant, I tell you truly, you are not unimportant in My eyes, and I have a great destiny for you as well!

I shall open up new ways and avenues to get My gospel out, and you shall travel them, My people. You shall be carriers of My glorious presence in the earth, as you walk in My ways and do what I have called you to do.

I shall do mighty exploits in the midst of you, My people. You shall be delighted and awestruck as you observe My miracle working power in your midst.

You that have obeyed Me and continued in My Word, who are truly My disciples, shall know great reward for your suffering this very year. Yes, your time has come for My mighty promises to be fulfilled in your lives. You have watched and waited faithfully. At times you wondered if I would manifest My promises at all. Now I shall.

This shall be a year of the transition of many nations. Many changes shall take place. Some will shock you. You will see My mighty hand at work in some of these. Hold on, for this ride shall be bumpy at times, My children; but many of you going in My Name shall hardly notice those changes for the change taking place in your own life, as I take you from glory to glory in My Holy Word, for you shall see some long desired changes manifesting in you.

I shall destroy the yokes of bondage off My people this year as they obey Me and continue in My Holy Word.

I shall remove some of those that affect you in your personal lives. Pray for them, My children, for their judgment shall be great if they continue refusing to repent. Pray for them diligently, for your prayers are heard in Heaven. They come up before My very throne and are of great value to Me, and you shall reap the rewards of them in your own lives there on earth.

Those of you who are ready to receive all I have for you, be in My Word <u>daily</u>. Study it and know it well, for a time approaches when it shall be a lifeline to you, and THOSE WHO DO NOT KNOW IT SHALL SUFFER GREATLY. As you study it, I shall touch you and change you, and you shall come to know Me as a very present help in times of trouble.

The times at hand shall trouble the people of the earth, but My people who abide in My Word, in whom My Word abides, shall not be so troubled, for they shall have Me—the Fountain of Living Waters—flowing to them and through them in these times. You must study My Word <u>daily</u> if you wish to receive My miracle working power, My children. I do not bestow it lightly. Do not say you know Me and then neglect your time with Me, FOR YOU SHALL KNOW ME NOT IF YOU NEGLECT MY WORD.

How can you witness to others of what you do not know of Me? There are many facets to Me—far more than you shall ever see in your time on earth, and I shall reveal many of them to you as you immerse yourself in My Holy Word.

Mark 16:15: And he said unto them, Go ye into all the world, and preach the gospel to every creature.

1 Peter 5:8: Be sober, be vigilant; because your adversary the devil, as a roaring lion, walketh about, seeking whom he may devour:

John 8:31: Then said Jesus to those Jews which believed on him, If ye continue in my Word, then are ye my disciples indeed;

2 Corinthians 3:18: But we all, with open face beholding as in a glass the glory of the Lord, are changed into the same image from glory to glory, even as by the Spirit of the Lord.

Isaiah 10:27: And it shall come to pass in that day, that his burden shall be taken away from off thy shoulder, and his yoke from off thy neck, and the yoke shall be destroyed because of the anointing.

Psalm 141:2: Let my prayer be set forth before thee as incense; and the lifting up of my hands as the evening sacrifice.

Psalm 1:2: But his delight is in the law of the LORD; and in his law doth he meditate day and night.

Matthew 4:4: But he answered and said, It is written, Man shall not live by bread alone, but by every Word that proceedeth out of the mouth of God.

2 Timothy 3:16-17: All scripture is given by inspiration of God, and is profitable for doctrine, for reproof, for correction, for instruction in righteousness: That the man of God may be perfect, thoroughly furnished unto all good works.

Romans 15:4: For whatsoever things were written aforetime were written for our learning, that we through patience and comfort of the scriptures might have hope.

Psalm 46:1: God is our refuge and strength, a very present help in trouble.

John 15:7: If ye abide in me, and my Words abide in you, ye shall ask what ye will, and it shall be done unto you.

Jeremiah 2:13: For my people have committed two evils; they have forsaken me the fountain of living waters, and hewed them out cisterns, broken cisterns, that can hold no water.

Jeremiah 17:13: O LORD, the hope of Israel, all that forsake thee shall be ashamed, and they that depart from me shall be written in the earth, because they have forsaken the LORD, the fountain of living waters.

1/05/2012

VISION OF THE WOUNDED LAMBS

I felt strongly led to worship late one night this week. I was in worship maybe ten minutes when a wave of grief hit me in the midsection. I felt the Father's sadness, and tears began to stream down my face as I began to pray in the Spirit, asking the Lord to reveal what the grief was from, in case anything in my life should have grieved Him so. I was shown this vision:

The vision opened to a very dark and dirty place. I saw a group of baby lambs there, and each was terribly wounded. He showed me in the Spirit that these are the lost ones, these are the ones no one has carried the Gospel to; and the darkness they are trapped in is of the enemy's making, and they do not have the knowledge of how to get free——the knowledge we carry.

Then I saw an arm come out of the darkness and in its hand was a big club. It began to beat one of the tiny lambs over and over with the giant club. Another arm appeared and began stabbing one of the other lambs, one that already had unhealed wounds on its small body when the stabbing began. The lambs were horribly wounded and crying, and there seemed to be no one in the dark place with them who even cared if they lived or died, or who cared that they were suffering so terribly.

The Lord showed me that these are the ones that are caught in the trap of addictions, and those are the ones trapped in abuse. The enemy has lied to them and kept them from the Lord with his lies. They struggled pitifully and looked so bewildered at what was happening to them. I could tell they were terrified, but they had no idea what to do.

By the time the vision ended, I was on my knees weeping, my heart completely broken by what I had seen happening to those tiny lambs, when the Lord began to speak:

Many of My people stand ready to rescue My lambs from the darkness, but they do not see a way. Tell them I will make a way for them to carry My gospel to the lost. I will move quickly, for little time is left before there will be no more chance to save them. The enemy has trapped them and chained them in the darkness.

My bride gorges herself at the table of the world's delights. Meanwhile, My people perish for lack of the knowledge of Me and My saving power.

I could hear His anger when He spoke of the filthy bride. As He spoke of her, I saw a woman in a filthy, torn wedding dress slouched back in a chair, devouring some kind of filth and nasty looking things from a big table that sat on the world. She acted like she had nothing better to do, and she did not seem to care that the filth was getting all over her face as she ate. She grabbed greedily and just kept cramming the filth into her mouth.

You are to be carriers of My power in the earth, My people! You are to go forth and preach My gospel to them while there is yet time. You must not waste any more time! Little time is left, and they are perishing, for the enemy has snared them.

I saw a steel trap in the Spirit like those used to trap animals, and Satan laughing as he approached to strike the last blow while the small animal crouched, terrified and unable to escape what was coming.

My people, you have been called for just such a time as this. It is not by accident you are where you are now. I have called you to preach My gospel. Why do you delay? I am about to make a way for you to go into dark places where My little ones are. I want you to obey Me and go. You have prayed to Me and asked to be used; now I am calling you forth.

I saw that the enemy was increasing his attacks against these lost ones, trying to get them into his kingdom before anyone could share the truth of the Gospel with them. He is launching major attacks at them—physical illness, financial problems, mental distress. The enemy is attempting to beat them down and wound them through others, until they lose hope and self-destruct through their addictions and abuse.

Do not delay. Souls are at stake, and My lambs perish because My bride is busy with the world. They are precious to Me, and I desire you would carry the message I give you to them.

Do not delay any longer. Time is passing quickly now, and there is no more time for playing in the world, My children. Do this for Me.

Rescue My lambs!

John 9:4: I must work the works of him that sent me, while it is day: the night cometh, when no man can work.

Hosea 4:6: My people are destroyed for lack of knowledge: because thou hast rejected knowledge, I will also reject thee, that thou shalt be no priest to me: seeing thou hast forgotten the law of thy God, I will also forget thy children.

Mark 16:15: And he said unto them, Go ye into all the world, and preach the gospel to every creature.

Esther 4:14: For if thou altogether holdest thy peace at this time, then shall there enlargement and deliverance arise to the Jews from another place; but thou and thy father's house shall be destroyed: and who knoweth whether thou art come to the kingdom for such a time as this?

1/12/12

BE NOT PUFFED UP

I had been praying to the Lord about the grief I felt because I was seeing so many Christians slandering and attacking other Christians. I was asking Him if He had anything to say to His people on the Blog Talk show that night when He spoke this to me:

I want to talk to My people about the attacks on other Christians. My people are called to walk in love, yet many of you think nothing of attacking My prophets, apostles, handmaidens, and servants. Do you not know I see your heart as you do this? Do you think I approve of your vicious attacks? Do you not see the damage you are doing to My body?

My people, the time has come for you to lay down the arms you have taken up against one another and use your weapons against the enemy of your souls. My people are busy fighting each other, and I desire they would fight the enemy instead.

Why do you waste time arguing doctrine while my lambs go unfed? (I could hear His anger when He said that!) *Why do you waste time pridefully believing you know all there is to know about My Word when you know nothing about love and walking in My ways? Is it more desirous that you know My Word or you walk in My ways?*

My children, stop arguing amongst yourselves. You live in a fallen world. You live amongst those who have been deceived by the enemy. You lie among the lost, the walking dead. Waste no more time jostling with each other. I desire you would reach out to the lost and hurting world around you in My love. I desire you would see the pain you have caused My little ones in the harshness of your words, for I do not consider it a small thing when you hurt one of My little ones. (I saw in this He meant those who have not grown much in the Word yet.)

I say lay down your arms against other believers today, or you shall face My judgment in these matters. You shall face consequences in your own lives for the destruction you are causing with the harshness of your words. (I saw that the Lord meant judgment NOW, not later—a reaping NOW of what is being sown.)

Be not puffed up in your knowledge of My Word, but walk in My ways and be a light in the lost and dying world in which you live. Be not a clanging cymbal in the ears of men, but sweet savor of love to Me instead. Do not go about sowing strife and calling it My work, for did I not say in My Word where strife and envying is, there will be also every evil work? Why then do you think you do My work when you sow strife among your brethren?

You err in pridefulness, My children. My face is against you in these matters, and you bring judgment upon your heads as you do them. Repent and turn from this wickedness. Repent and love the brethren as I have instructed you in My Word.

John 13:35: By this shall all men know that ye are my disciples, if ye have love one to another.

John 21:15: So when they had dined, Jesus saith to Simon Peter, Simon, son of Jonas, lovest thou me more than these? He saith unto him, Yea, Lord; thou knowest that I love thee. He saith unto him, Feed my lambs.

1 Peter 3:8: Finally, be ye all of one mind, having compassion one of another, love as brethren, be pitiful, be courteous:

Matthew 18:11: For the Son of man is come to save that which was lost.

1 Corinthians 13:4: Charity suffereth long, and is kind; charity envieth not; charity vaunteth not itself, is not puffed up.

1 Peter 3:12: For the eyes of the Lord are over the righteous, and his ears are open unto their prayers: but the face of the Lord is against them that do evil.

Psalm 105:15: Saying, Touch not mine anointed, and do my prophets no harm.

Proverbs 6:16-19: These six things doth the LORD hate: yea, seven are an abomination unto him: A proud look, a lying tongue, and hands that shed innocent blood, An heart that deviseth wicked imaginations, feet that be swift in running to mischief, A false witness that speaketh lies, and he that soweth discord among brethren.

Proverbs 8:13: The fear of the LORD is to hate evil: pride, and arrogancy, and the evil way, and the froward mouth, do I hate.

Proverbs 16:18: Pride goeth before destruction, and an haughty spirit before a fall.

1 Corinthians 13:1: Though I speak with the tongues of men and of angels, and have not charity, I am become as sounding brass, or a tinkling cymbal.

1/18/12

WHY DO YOU PLAY STILL?

It was very late tonight, almost 3 a.m., and I was reading the Word when I felt strongly the Lord wanted me to pray in the Spirit. I prayed for some minutes, and then the Lord spoke this message to me:

The enemy desires to sift you as wheat, My children. Do you not see the times at hand? Do you not know what hour it has become? Why do you not make yourselves ready for My Son's return to the earth? Why do you play still in the world and neglect your time with Me and your time in My Word?

All My children who neglect these things shall suffer terrible consequences in times to come. You do not realize all that is about to happen My little ones, and I cannot reveal all to you, but heed My warning:

DO NOT NEGLECT YOUR TIME WITH ME, NOR YOUR TIME IN MY HOLY WORD, FOR THEN YOU SHALL TRULY BE UNPREPARED FOR ALL THAT IS ABOUT TO TRANSPIRE IN THE EARTH.

Psalm 119:105: Thy Word is a lamp unto my feet, and a light unto my path.

2 Timothy 3:16-17: All scripture is given by inspiration of God, and is profitable for doctrine, for reproof, for correction, for instruction in righteousness: That the man of God may be perfect, thoroughly furnished unto all good works.

Matthew 4:4: But he answered and said, It is written, Man shall not live by bread alone, but by every Word that proceedeth out of the mouth of God.

Joshua 1:8: This Book of the Law shall not depart from your mouth, but you shall meditate on it day and night, so that you may be careful to do according to all that is written in it. For then you will make your way prosperous, and then you will have good success.

1/26/12

SEEK ME FOR I SHALL BE FOUND

I was reading the Word in 2 Chronicles 17 about the various wars kings have won and lost when the Lord began speaking to me:

See what I have done?

Yes, Lord. When they obeyed, You prospered them and fought for them. When they sinned, You didn't. How do people not see the connection between obedience and blessing, Lord? How can they not see it? Your Word says You change not—You are the same today as You were back then.

It's not that they can't see it. They don't want to. They like their sinful state of being, and hope I will overlook it as ignorance on the Day of Judgment, but it shall not be so, daughter. (I heard a terrible sadness in His voice when He said that.)

They shall pay for the sins they choose not to forsake. Warn them, daughter! Tell My people their sins are grievous in My eyes, and I do not look lightly on those who choose the pleasures of the flesh over Me and My ways. I have provided in My Word a way out of your sins, My people. There is now no excuse—except you want to continue sinning—for why you are not free.

Seek Me, for I shall be found by you and will give you the keys to your deliverance if only you will seek My face and not the pleasures of the world instead. This world shall pass away, but I will never pass away. The treasures in My Holy Word will never pass away.

You can be free if you will choose freedom, if you will choose Me, for I shall make you free. Seek Me, for I shall be found of you if you will seek Me. Come to Me as a little child, believing with all your heart, My children.

Do not believe the enemy's words that you can never be free, for did I not say in My Holy Word that he is a liar and the father of lies? Why then do you allow him to speak to you so? Why do you choose to believe him over Me?

I desire for you to be free, little ones. Free indeed! Free and rejoicing in your Father's Mighty Power. Free to share your testimony far and wide of all I have done in you.

I desire the enemy would have no part in you, that you would not listen to his taunts and lies, that you would instead look at My Word for truth to replace them.

Come away from the fires of temptation, My children, for your enemy seeks to destroy you through the lusts of your flesh.

John 3:19: And this is the condemnation, that light is come into the world, and men loved darkness rather than light, because their deeds were evil.

James 4:8: Draw nigh to God, and he will draw nigh to you. Cleanse your hands, ye sinners; and purify your hearts, ye double minded.

John 8:44: Ye are of your father the devil, and the lusts of your father ye will do. He was a murderer from the beginning, and abode not in the truth, because there is no truth in him. When he speaketh a lie, he speaketh of his own: for he is a liar, and the father of it.

John 8:36: If the Son therefore shall make you free, ye shall be free indeed.

1 Peter 5:8: Be sober, be vigilant; because your adversary the devil, as a roaring lion, walketh about, seeking whom he may devour.

John 10:10: The thief cometh not, but for to steal, and to kill, and to destroy: I am come that they might have life, and that they might have it more abundantly.

2/5/12

I WILL GIVE YOU THE KEYS

I was in prayer about a type of ministry I desire to see spring up in the place where I live when the Lord began to speak to me and show me some of the reasons why He called me to the city He told me to move to here in Texas. As I was praying, He spoke this Word to me:

My people do not realize the importance of the places in which I have placed them in this time. They know not the plans I have for them, for they are busy seeking about them for provision, provision which they need not search for if only they will seek My face instead.

My people, the enemy has deceived you into thinking you must make your own way in this world, when I have a better plan for you. I have placed you where you are for a season for a reason; and that reason will be revealed to you if you will only seek Me for it. IF YOU IGNORE MY PLAN FOR YOU IN THAT PLACE, MY

BLESSINGS WILL NOT FLOW READILY TO YOU, and you will miss some of what I have for you.

Seek Me for your purpose. Seek Me about your destiny. Seek Me, for I shall be found by you and I will reveal to you what you need to know. Do not go seeking others for this knowledge, but seek Me and trust Me to tell you in My ways and times.

You feel empty and lost because you are not walking in My ways and reasons for where you are. You feel alone, for I have you alone so you will more readily seek My face.

Seek Me, for I shall be found by you. Do not look to the world for your answers. Do not seek out people to give you the reasons but seek Me, your Maker, for My plan, for only I know truly what I have called each of you to do. I, only, hold the keys to your destiny.

Seek Me, and I will give you the keys to unlock your destiny in Me.

Psalm 46:10: Be still, and know that I am God: I will be exalted among the heathen, I will be exalted in the earth.

Eccl. 3:1: To everything there is a season, and a time to every purpose under the heaven.

Jeremiah 29:13: And ye shall seek me, and find me, when ye shall search for me with all your heart.

Mathew 7:7: Ask, and it shall be given to you; seek, and ye shall find; knock, and it shall be opened unto you.

2/9/12

I AM STIRRING UP NATIONS

I am stirring up nations to fight against nations and peoples to war within themselves. I am stirring up households where unbelief remains. I will cause My people to choose Me or choose the world by increasing the strife among them.

My people have been lax in their choices to serve Me, preferring comfort and routine to zeal for My house, so I am stirring them up. I will cause you to choose Me, My people, or be lost to Me forever by the way you choose in what is soon to come.

Nation shall rise up against nation and groups of nations against a nation, and I shall cause you to choose. What you see will strike fear in your heart, yet you need fear only Me and My mighty Hand of Judgment. Choose Me and My ways and live.

As turmoil increases around you, you must choose Me. As persecutions arise, you must choose Me and My ways over your own. There is no room for compromise on the narrow path. Those who do not know Me will not survive what is coming for long, for there shall be no earthly remedy to help them.

Many will see things they have not seen before and fear, for this is a time like none that has come before it. Truly I tell you, great fear shall rise up in men's hearts in what is to come, for methods and foundations gone before shall fail them.

As turmoil in the earth increases, persecution shall arise like never before. A people shall rise against My people to do them injustice. My people shall cry out to Me, and I shall deliver them speedily.

Consider your ways, My people. Consider well the choices you have made and are making, for this shall come upon you quickly. Those who are not rooted and grounded in Me shall be blown about by events in the earth, but My people shall stand firm.

Consider your ways and choose wisely, for you live in a time like no other, and these choices cannot be undone. Many shall perish suddenly in events coming, and there shall be no remedy for them.

Those who are not with Me are against Me.

Be found in Me. Be found in My ways. Be not afraid, only believe.

Romans 11:21: For if God spared not the natural branches, take heed lest he also spare not thee.

Ephesians 6:13-15: Wherefore take unto you the whole armour of God, that ye may be able to withstand in the evil day, and having done all, to stand. Stand therefore, having your loins girt about with truth, and having on the breastplate of righteousness; And your feet shod with the preparation of the gospel of peace.

Matthew 10:34-37: Think not that I am come to send peace on earth: I came not to send peace, but a sword. For I am come to set a man at variance against his father, and the daughter against her mother, and the daughter-in-law against her mother-in- law. And a man's foes shall be they of his own household. He that loveth father or mother more than me is not worthy of me: and he that loveth son or daughter more than me is not worthy of me.

Matthew 24:7: For nation shall rise against nation, and kingdom against kingdom: and there shall be famines, and pestilences, and earthquakes, in divers places.

Luke 21:26: Men's hearts failing them for fear, and for looking after those things which are coming on the earth: for the powers of heaven shall be shaken.

John 15:18: If the world hate you, ye know that it hated me before it hated you.

2 Timothy 3:12: Yea, and all that will live godly in Christ Jesus shall suffer persecution.

2/18/12

THE MEAT GRINDER VISION

I was in worship, and a vision appeared to me of something that resembled a meat grinder with a funnel on top. I saw a man go into the top of the funnel and drop down into the meat grinder, and it began grinding. I began to see small pieces of hard substances fly out of the grinder as it was grinding. I saw that the man was going through terrible pain and adversity and many difficult situations while he was in the grinder. Then I heard the words, "Threshing Floor."

I saw that none of the fluffy teachings the man had heard could withstand the terrible pressure of the meat grinder, and they quickly flew away out the top. As I watched, I was shown that the people who were in the meat grinder were those who had laid down the most for the Kingdom of God. When the grinder stopped, the man dropped out of the chute at the bottom, but he looked different. He was stronger, wearing very shiny armor, and he was smiling and really happy. I then heard the word, "Equipped."

Off to the side, I could see others who had laid down less were also going through things. I saw some being pounded by meat tenderizing mallets, some very hard, and some not so hard. They would cry out as the mallet came down on them, but the gentle hand wielding the mallet continued to pound. I knew in my spirit when I saw this, that things were being worked out of them by the pounding.

I felt strongly the Lord had something to say to us about what He was showing me, and I began to pray that He would reveal it. This is what He said:

Yes, My daughter, many of My children who have been called to My Kingdom work are now on My threshing floor. I am separating from them all that does not please Me and making them meet for My use.

These are those who have submitted themselves wholly to Me for My purposes, and great shall be their reward, for the works they shall now do shall glorify My Son in the earth.

A time of great darkness approaches in the earth when no man shall know or understand all that is occurring. Few will see My purposes in what is to come. Only My children who have walked with Me through seasons of darkness will understand and know how to acclimate themselves in that time. In that time there shall be great turmoil, great need, and much uncertainty. It shall be the darkest of times.

I shall give My children who are walking close to Me eyes to see in the darkness. I SHALL GIVE THEM GREAT AND MIGHTY REVELATIONS THAT THEY MAY SURVIVE WHAT IS TO COME. I shall provide for them and protect them and keep all that is theirs, that they may tell others of My great faithfulness.

There is nothing you need do, My children, to prepare for what is coming, for I am able to provide all you need. Walk with Me; Seek My face daily. Do not neglect your time with Me or be led astray by the distractions of the world, for the world cannot save you from what is to come.

Go forth, speak My Word. Tell others of your God who is mighty to save and deliver. Watch and pray, for this time quickly approaches.

2 Timothy 2:20-21: But in a great house there are not only vessels of gold and of silver, but also of wood and of earth; and some to honour, and some to dishonour.

If a man therefore purge himself from these, he shall be a vessel unto honour, sanctified, and meet for the master's use, and prepared unto every good work.

Mark 16:15: And he said unto them, Go ye into all the world, and preach the gospel to every creature.

Mark 13:33: Take ye heed, watch and pray: for ye know not when the time is.

Isaiah 55:6-7: Seek ye the LORD while he may be found, call ye upon him while he is near: Let the wicked forsake his way, and the unrighteous man his thoughts: and let him return unto the LORD, and he will have mercy upon him; and to our God, for he will abundantly pardon.

3/5/12

A THROWAWAY GOD

Many have let their guard down now as the economy has shown signs of life again, feeling they no longer need Me, but they are mistaken.

My people, do you not know? Do you not see what is happening around you? Will you never learn to stop wavering like thin reeds in the breeze? Do you not see that I am not a throwaway God, like something you pick up at a convenience store and dispose of when it is no longer needed?

Now that your economy looks better, you feel the danger is past and you can relax, but woe to those who so easily turn away from Me, the Fount of Living Water, for your destruction comes upon you suddenly and without warning! I have given you space to repent, but you have quickly turned to the pleasures of the world once again, thinking you have no need of Me now.

Woe unto you, for you shall be like Sodom and Gomorrah in that day, for no other sign shall be given to you who are of a double heart. YOU SHALL BE QUICKLY TAKEN FROM THE EARTH WHEN MY JUDGMENTS FALL UPON YOUR HEAD.

I love you, My children, with an everlasting love, but I will not tolerate unfaithfulness in your hearts. I show Myself faithful to you; show yourselves faithful to Me also. I desire you would come to Me every day, seek My face every day—not only when you have need of My power in your lives! Then shall I be able to protect you from what is coming in the earth.

Jeremiah 2:13: For my people have committed two evils; they have forsaken me the fountain of living waters, and hewed them out cisterns, broken cisterns, that can hold no water.

Rev. 2:21: And I gave her space to repent of her fornication; and she repented not.

Deut. 29:22-24: So that the generation to come of your children that shall rise up after you, and the stranger that shall come from a far land, shall say, when they see the plagues of that land, and the sicknesses which the LORD hath laid upon it; And that the whole land thereof is brimstone, and salt, and burning, that it is not sown, nor beareth, nor any grass groweth therein, like the overthrow of Sodom, and Gomorrah, Admah, and Zeboim, which the LORD overthrew in his anger, and

in his wrath: Even all nations shall say, Wherefore hath the LORD done thus unto this land? what meaneth the heat of this great anger?

Deut. 7:9: Know therefore that the LORD thy God, he is God, the faithful God, which keepeth covenant and mercy with them that love him and keep his commandments to a thousand generations.

3/8/12

THIS YEAR

My people, you are stubborn against Me in your way of doing things. I have pleaded with you about walking with Me closely, yet you hear Me not. You have itching ears to hear only the messages you wish to hear, the messages that tickle your ears and delight your flesh, but these are not the words you are in need of now.

Much is approaching in the world you know not of and are not prepared for yet. You are not yet ready to face the end of all things as you know them, yet you go along your way as though you were.

Time is growing short and you must prepare for what lies ahead. Why have you not sought My face diligently for the knowledge you shall require in that time? Did you think My words were only for others and not you also?

Why do you show Me no worship when you know this I desire of you? I desire you would draw near to Me each day in worship and adoration. What is soon to come will terrify many of you, and you will be among them if you are not prepared by being in My presence daily. It will be unlike anything you have ever witnessed before now. DRAW NEAR TO ME THAT I MAY INSTRUCT YOU ON WHAT YOU SHALL NEED IN THAT TIME, AND YOU WILL BE PREPARED.

I desire My people would believe Me more for lost souls. I desire you would begin to truly believe Me to move the hearts of your unsaved loved ones, for I desire to save them.

This year I will save many others have given up on. Those you think will never turn to Me will be saved if you will only believe. I desire intercession from My people. Intercede with faith that I will save those you love, and My hand shall move mightily in response to your prayers!

This year I shall turn many hard hearts to Me.

This year I desire My glory would abound in the earth—that My people would move in signs and in wonders, that others may believe on Me and have life everlasting. I desire you would believe Me for more, for My arm is not too short to save, to heal, to deliver.

Begin now believing Me for more, My people, for I am a mighty God who is well able to deliver all you can believe Me for, and far more. You have been limiting Me with your small faith. Begin to believe for impossible things, for what is impossible for you is easy for Me. With Me, all things are possible. This year I desire to move mightily in the earth among My people and among unbelievers.

I will send angelic messages to some of My chosen this year. THEY WILL BEAR MY INSTRUCTIONS. Watch for them.

Time is growing short, My children. Get ready. Be prepared. Watch and pray.

Believe Me to do what you cannot.

John 4:23: But the hour cometh, and now is, when the true worshippers shall worship the Father in Spirit and in truth: for the Father seeketh such to worship him.

Isaiah 59:1: Behold, the LORD's hand is not shortened, that it cannot save; neither his ear heavy that it cannot hear:

Psalm 72:19: And blessed be his glorious name for ever: and let the whole earth be filled with his glory; Amen and Amen.

Luke 1:37: For with God nothing shall be impossible.

Mark 13:33: Take ye heed, watch and pray: for ye know not when the time is.

3/15/12

WANT OF GAIN

The time has now come for My righteous ones to be exalted. In days past, those who appeared righteous have risen high. Not so now, for I shall exalt those truly found righteous in My sight. I am the Lord, the great Judge of all. I judge the hearts and reins of all people.

Many of your leaders appeared righteous in your eyes who were vile in My sight. Their hearts were black with want of gain and their thoughts of profit.

I will exalt My righteous ones who daily seek My face, those whose hearts are truly to do My will. No more shall the greedy be exalted, for I shall judge them one by one, and you shall see them fall from their lofty perches.

(Speaking to those greedy ones here) *No more shall you prey on My precious widows and poor saints, for I shall turn My face from you and withdraw My hand of protection from all you do. You will turn to Me with weeping in that day when your kingdom falls before you.*

Wash you, make you clean! Purify your hearts before Me, the Holy One of Israel, that you may be spared in that terrible Day of Judgment, that I may show you mercy.

Turn again and restore that which was taken away from My people, that I may show you mercy now.

Psalm 7:9: Oh let the wickedness of the wicked come to an end; but establish the just: for the righteous God trieth the hearts and reins.

Psalm 75:10: All the horns of the wicked also will I cut off; but the horns of the righteous shall be exalted.

Jeremiah 17:9-10: The heart is deceitful above all things, and desperately wicked: who can know it? I the LORD search the heart, I try the reins, even to give every man according to his ways, and according to the fruit of his doings.

Isaiah 2:11-12: The lofty looks of man shall be humbled, and the haughtiness of men shall be bowed down, and the LORD alone shall be exalted in that day. For the day of the LORD of hosts shall be upon every one that is proud and lofty, and upon every one that is lifted up; and he shall be brought low.

Isaiah 10:1-3: Woe unto them that decree unrighteous decrees, and that write grievousness which they have prescribed; To turn aside the needy from judgment, and to take away the right from the poor of my people, that widows may be their prey, and that they may rob the fatherless! And what will ye do in the day of visitation, and in the desolation which shall come from far? to whom will ye flee for help? and where will ye leave your glory?

Isaiah 1:15-17: And when ye spread forth your hands, I will hide mine eyes from you: yea, when ye make many prayers, I will not hear: your hands are full of blood. Wash you, make you clean; put away the evil of your doings from before mine eyes; cease to do evil; Learn to do well; seek judgment, relieve the oppressed, judge the fatherless, plead for the widow.

Joel 2:11-13: And the LORD shall utter his voice before his army: for his camp is very great: for he is strong that executeth his Word: for the day of the LORD is great and very terrible; and who can abide it? Therefore also now, saith the LORD, turn ye even to me with all your heart, and with fasting, and with weeping, and with mourning: And rend your heart, and not your garments, and turn unto the LORD your God: for he is gracious and merciful, slow to anger, and of great kindness, and repenteth him of the evil.

Hebrews 12:22-27: But ye are come unto mount Sion, and unto the city of the living God, the heavenly Jerusalem, and to an innumerable company of angels, To the general assembly and church of the firstborn, which are written in heaven, and to God the Judge of all, and to the spirits of just men made perfect, And to Jesus the mediator of the new covenant, and to the blood of sprinkling, that speaketh better things than that of Abel. See that ye refuse not him that speaketh. For if they escaped not who refused him that spake on earth, much more shall not we escape, if we turn away from him that speaketh from heaven: Whose voice then shook the earth: but now he hath promised, saying, Yet once more I shake not the earth only, but also heaven. And this word, Yet once more, signifieth the removing of those things that are shaken, as of things that are made, that those things which cannot be shaken may remain.

3/15/12

UNIONS NOT OF ME

I was listening on the phone to a friend talking about recent changes in her marriage this week, and how she and her husband went from almost filing for divorce to attending church together, and the new love that was blossoming between them as a result, when the Lord showed me something in my spirit.

He showed me that He is shaking the marriages where there is a true believer that is yoked with one who believes little or not at all, and He is shaking them hard, so that the one who does not really believe or is in unbelief will either start following Him, or the believer will be set free.

Later that night during worship, He spoke this Word to me:

Relationships will be tried by fire in this time. What is not of Me shall not survive the test of My refining fire. In what is coming, your unions must be pure.

Many of you will experience loss in this time of refining. Know that I will restore to My people what is rightfully theirs and cause you to increase more besides.

I AM CAUSING UNBELIEVERS TO CHOOSE NOW. I have come to set My people free in this time from all that keeps them from serving Me with their whole hearts. I will now remove the obstacles and move My people strategically into position for that which is very soon to come. **Unions not of Me cannot withstand the storm that is coming.**

DO NOT BE SURPRISED WHEN YOU SEE LONGSTANDING UNIONS CRUMBLE OVERNIGHT, for this is My mighty hand.

I am preparing you, My people. I will care for you in times to come. Have no fear, for I am a loving and faithful Father. Many of you shall fear as events planned begin to come to pass, but these things must come that My Name might be glorified in all the earth before My Son's soon return.

Psalm 127:1: Except the LORD build the house, they labour in vain that build it: except the LORD keep the city, the watchman waketh but in vain.

2 Cor. 6:14: Be ye not unequally yoked together with unbelievers: for what fellowship hath righteousness with unrighteousness? and what communion hath light with darkness?

Malachi 3:2-3: But who may abide the day of his coming? and who shall stand when he appeareth? for he is like a refiner's fire, and like fullers' soap: And he shall sit as a refiner and purifier of silver: and he shall purify the sons of Levi, and purge them as gold and silver, that they may offer unto the LORD an offering in righteousness.

Joel 2:25: And I will restore to you the years that the locust hath eaten, the cankerworm, and the caterpillar, and the palmerworm, my great army which I sent among you.

Psalm 23:3: He restoreth my soul: he leadeth me in the paths of righteousness for his name's sake.

3/20/12

THE SHAKING IS BEGINNING

A few days ago, as I was waking up, I saw another vision of things shaking. I saw myself standing in the midst of many tall buildings. Then the buildings all began shaking and some began to break down under the intensity of the shaking that was taking place. The intensity did not lessen, but continued.

I heard the words *"Walk in My ways."*

I began to pray and ask the Lord why I see vision after vision of things being shaken. He answered.

I will shake the economic, then the spiritual, then what is under the ground, when I arise and shake terribly the earth.

Today, I was again praying about the shaking, and He spoke again.

The shaking is beginning, My people. You will now see many things around you begin to shake. Everything from relationships to governments to belief systems shall be shaken in this time. What is not of Me shall not stand the test of shaking.

Strengthen your faith, My children. Know that I will protect and provide for you in coming times, and do not doubt. Believe only, for this is the key to receiving anything from My mighty hand. Believe in Me.

Mark 5:36: As soon as Jesus heard the word that was spoken, he saith unto the ruler of the synagogue, Be not afraid, only believe.

Isaiah 2:19: And they shall go into the holes of the rocks, and into the caves of the earth, for fear of the LORD, and for the glory of his majesty, when he ariseth to shake terribly the earth.

Matther 6:32-34: For after all these things do the Gentiles seek: for your heavenly Father knoweth that you have need of all these things. But seek ye first the kingdom of God, and his righteousness; and all these things shall be added unto you. Take therefore no thought for the morrow: for the morrow shall take thought for the things of itself. Sufficient unto the day is the evil thereof.

3/28/12

RELEASE WHAT IS NO LONGER USEFUL

The Lord had been speaking to me about clearing the clutter out of my work space and getting rid of old things and getting my house in order, and I was praying over what He wanted me to do when He began to speak this Word to me:

Tell My children the time has come for them to release the old and step into the new I have for them. Many of My children cling to the old in their lives because they fear loss. They fear regret, and they fear doing without. They are not trusting Me, the Holy One of Israel, for all things, as I desire for them to do.

My children, do you not know the lateness of the hour? Do you not know all I have called you to accomplish in this hour? DO YOU NOT SEE THAT YOU CANNOT MOVE FORWARD WHILE CLINGING TO THE PAST? You must release what is no longer useful in your lives, to Me.

Trust Me to complete the good works I have begun in you in this time. Do not stand idly by, but do not fear either. Walk hand in hand with Me, and I shall accomplish all I desire in you.

MANY OF YOU ARE IN SITUATIONS I DID NOT INTEND FOR YOU, WHICH ARE OF YOUR OWN MAKING. Listen carefully for My voice and leading on how to proceed, that I may bring you to a place of fullness of purpose and blessing.

Matthew 9:16: No man putteth a piece of new cloth unto an old garment, for that which is put in to fill it up taketh from the garment, and the rent is made worse.

Luke 5:39: No man also having drunk old wine straightway desireth new: for he saith, The old is better.

2 Timothy 1:7: For God hath not given us the spirit of fear; but of power, and of love, and of a sound mind.

Phil. 3:13: Brethren, I count not myself to have apprehended: but this one thing I do, forgetting those things which are behind, and reaching forth unto those things which are before,

Luke 9:62: And Jesus said unto him, No man, having put his hand to the plough, and looking back, is fit for the kingdom of God.

4/6/12

PREPARE FOR WAR

Prepare for war in your land, My people, for this generation shall pay for all the innocent blood that has been shed by those before you. Your children and grandchildren also shall pay the price for the sins of your lands, for the end is near and judgment is upon all lands.

LIFE AS YOU KNOW IT SHALL NO MORE BE, for My mouth has spoken it. I, the Holy One of Israel, have decreed, and so it shall be.

Gen. 4:19: And he said, What hast thou done? the voice of thy brother's blood crieth unto me from the ground.

Gen. 9:6: Whoso sheddeth man's blood, by man shall his blood be shed: for in the image of God made he man.

Deut. 19:10: That innocent blood be not shed in thy land, which the LORD thy God giveth thee for an inheritance, and so blood be upon thee.

Prov. 6:16-18: These six things doth the LORD hate: yea, seven are an abomination unto him: A proud look, a lying tongue, and hands that shed innocent blood, An heart that deviseth wicked imaginations, feet that be swift in running to mischief,

Hab. 2:8: Because thou hast spoiled many nations, all the remnant of the people shall spoil thee; because of men's blood, and for the violence of the land, of the city, and of all that dwell therein.

Psalm 106:36-38: And they served their idols: which were a snare unto them. Yea, they sacrificed their sons and their daughters unto devils, And shed innocent blood, even the blood of their sons and of their daughters, whom they sacrificed unto the idols of Canaan: and the land was polluted with blood.

Isaiah 59:7: Their feet run to evil, and they make haste to shed innocent blood: their thoughts are thoughts of iniquity; wasting and destruction are in their paths.

Jer. 32:18: Thou showest loving kindness unto thousands, and recompensest the iniquity of the fathers into the bosom of their children after them: the Great, the Mighty God, the LORD of hosts, is his name.

Ezekiel 35:6: Therefore, as I live, saith the Lord GOD, I will prepare thee unto blood, and blood shall pursue thee: sith thou hast not hated blood, even blood shall pursue thee.

Joel 3:19: Egypt shall be a desolation, and Edom shall be a desolate wilderness, for the violence against the children of Judah, because they have shed innocent blood in their land.

Psalm 91

1. He that dwelleth in the secret place of the most High shall abide under the shadow of the Almighty. 2. I will say of the LORD, He is my refuge and my fortress: my God; in him will I trust. 3. Surely he shall deliver thee from the snare of the fowler, and from the noisome pestilence. 4. He shall cover thee with his feathers, and under his wings shalt thou trust: his truth shall be thy shield and buckler. 5. Thou shalt not be afraid for the terror by night; nor for the arrow that flieth by day; 6. Nor for the pestilence that walketh in darkness; nor for the destruction that wasteth at noonday. 7. A thousand shall fall at thy side, and ten thousand at thy right hand; but it shall not come nigh thee. 8. Only with thine eyes shalt thou behold and see the reward of the wicked. 9. Because thou hast made the LORD, which is my refuge, even the most High, thy habitation; 10. There shall no evil befall thee, neither shall any plague come nigh thy dwelling. 11. For he shall give his angels charge over thee, to keep thee in all thy ways. 12. They shall bear thee up in their hands, lest thou dash thy foot against a stone. 13. Thou shalt tread upon the lion and adder: the young lion and the dragon shalt thou trample under feet. 14. Because he hath set his love upon me, therefore will I deliver him: I will set him on high, because he hath known my name. 15. He shall call upon me, and I will answer him: I will be with him in trouble; I will deliver him, and honour him. 16. With long life will I satisfy him, and show him my salvation.

4/13/12

A TIME OF MANY TRANSITIONS

My children, you are in a time of many transitions. You are transitioning between the former Age and this one, and many of you feel uncertain because of this. I am shaking everything that can be shaken, and many of you are feeling it. Anything that is not sure and founded on Me and My Word, I will shake. I am shaking relationships, jobs, careers, health, belief systems. I am shaking everything which concerns you to show you what is not of Me. Many of you struggle against the shaking because you do not understand what it is I am doing. Find your peace about these matters in Me, and trust Me to take care of you no matter what happens.

All that has been sacred in your lives is subject to change. Only I do not change, all else is fleeting. Find your security in Me. Find your assurance in Me.

Do not struggle against this thing that I do, for it is to your benefit that I do it. Now is the time all must be tested, for what is not of Me cannot withstand what is soon to come.

Unions not of Me will not stand.
Homes not built on Me will not stand.
Relationships not built on Me will not stand.

I no longer bless and support what is not of Me. When you see these things fall, it is because I have removed My hand from them. Nations not of Me will not stand. Be found in Me that you may stand in the times to come. Go forth, spread My Word, My glorious gospel, and be blessed. All that is not of Me shall soon perish.

If your knowledge is complete in My Word, then you will not be moved. Anything that is not in line with My Word in your life will be subject to My shaking. I am raising My children up to new levels in this age. You cannot hold on to the dead and dry things of the world, to relationships not of Me, on the way to where you are going. I shall empower you to release all the enemy has burdened you with that is not My will for you.

Many of you cling to the former things when I desire to give you something new. You cling to what you know, for you see no other way; but I am the way-maker, and I make the way for My children to walk in health, to prosper in all the fullness of Me, to have right relationships that honor Me and bring glory to My Name. You cling to old things because nothing new is in sight, but I desire you would release the old to Me and allow Me to work My will in it.

Praise Me in and for all things, whether you understand them or not, for this is what I desire of you. When you do not understand a loss that has occurred, trust that I know the plan, for I am the truth, the life, and the way for you.

Whenever you do not know the way, look to Me, for I am the way. If you need life in your body, call on My Name, for I am the life-giver. If you need the truth about any situation, look into My Holy Word, for it will speak truth to you at all times, and all answers are contained therein, if you will only seek them.

Seek Me. Know Me. Trust Me.

Trust that I know and do what is best for you and your life and the lives of My other children at all times, and do not fear. Do not fear as you see My judgments falling in your nations, My children, for these things must surely come to pass. My Word shall be fulfilled to the last letter before My return and before the end comes, and the end is near now.

Look up, My children, for your redemption draweth nigh. Rejoice! For your time on earth is short now, as all that is contained in My Word is being brought to pass. Finish your journeys with faith and great courage, for your reward shall be great indeed if you do this.

I love you with an everlasting love, and I am watching over you as this Age comes to a close.

Psalm 92:1: It is a good thing to give thanks unto the Lord, and to sing praises unto Thy name, O Most High.

John 14:6: Jesus saith unto him, I am the way, the truth, and the life: no man cometh unto the Father, but by me.

Psalm 32:10: Many sorrows shall be to the wicked: but he that trusteth in the LORD, mercy shall compass him about.

Psalm 37:5: Commit thy way unto the LORD; trust also in him; and he shall bring it to pass.

Acts 2:21: And it shall come to pass that whosoever shall call on the name of the Lord shall be saved.

Luke 21:28: And when these things begin to come to pass, then look up, and lift up your heads; for your redemption draweth nigh.

5/3/12

CHAINED

I was deep in worship, adoring the Lord, when chains appeared on my hands, then on my feet, then shackles appeared on my legs. I began to cry out and beg Him to break the chains off me, and He began to speak this message.

My bride has enslaved herself to the world and its ways. I desire that she would free herself, but she would not, for she has preferred the pleasures of the flesh over all I can give to her.

In the Spirit, I saw the world and all the people there. At first they were all walking towards the world, and then some began to turn back and worship the King of Kings. As the group that had turned back worshiped Him, I saw golden oil pouring down from Heaven onto them from His hand. As they worshiped, the group that kept walking towards the world groaned heavily as they continued moving further into darkness and chaos.

My bride's chains are forged in her own sins, and she refuses to lay them down, though I have already set her free and ordained her freedom from sin.

I have called to My children again and again, but they turn not, and now judgment must come to the earth. Those who will not turn from sin shall perish, for the wages of sin is death, My children.

Why do you prefer darkness over light? For I withhold no good thing from those who serve Me and walk in My ways, yet you refuse and continue in bondage. You no longer cry out for freedom, for you have found comfort in your sins and prefer them to Me and My ways. This is truly grievous in My eyes.

In the Spirit, I saw that as the people in chains sinned, their chains became heavier and heavier.

Every act, every deed of darkness, adds to your chains. Do you not see your bondage? Do you not feel the weight of your sins and long to be free to serve Me with your whole heart? You have cast Me aside like an old lover and taken up with the world. (When He said that, I heard a great grieving sadness in His voice.)

The Evil One comes for you, My children, and those under heavy weight of sin shall not be able to escape him in time.

Turn now—turn to Me and cry out, and I shall make you free.

Romans 6:16: Know ye not, that to whom ye yield yourselves servants to obey, his servants ye are to whom ye obey; whether of sin unto death, or of obedience unto righteousness?

2 Corinthians 6:14: Be ye not unequally yoked together with unbelievers: for what fellowship hath righteousness with unrighteousness? and what communion hath light with darkness?

Psalm 84:11: For the LORD God is a sun and shield: the LORD will give grace and glory: no good thing will he withhold from them that walk uprightly.

John 8:34: Jesus answered them, Verily, verily, I say unto you, Whosoever committeth sin is the servant of sin.

Luke 5:32: I came not to call the righteous, but sinners to repentance.

John 8:36: If the Son therefore shall make you free, ye shall be free indeed.

Acts 3:19: Repent ye therefore, and be converted, that your sins may be blotted out, when the times of refreshing shall come from the presence of the Lord.

Romans 6:23: For the wages of sin is death; but the gift of God is eternal life through Jesus Christ our Lord.

James 4:4: Ye adulterers and adulteresses, know ye not that the friendship of the world is enmity with God? whosoever therefore will be a friend of the world is the enemy of God.

Ephesians 5:27: That he might present it to himself a glorious church, not having spot, or wrinkle, or any such thing; but that it should be holy and without blemish.

2 Peter 2:9: The Lord knoweth how to deliver the godly out of temptations, and to reserve the unjust unto the day of judgment to be punished.

5/10/12

AMERICA, AMERICA

Oh America, America, why do you fight for what is wrong and abandon those who speak what is right? So shall you be left desolate in the Day of your Judgments.

You claim to know what is right, yet you do what is wrong in the darkness of your chambers. In your heart is only blackness, and no mercy shall be shown you in that Day.

I shall bring another, great and mighty, to tear you to pieces. It shall crush you under its feet and trample your beauty, and you shall be no more.

You refuse to show mercy, and so shall you be refused mercy in your time of destruction.

Woe to you who call evil good and good evil and who seek your own glory at the price of others' heads. So shall your own head have a price among the nations, and you shall be hunted and destroyed.

Prepare, My people, for the end of America looms near. She has many enemies who secretly want to see her brought down, and so shall it be done, for the Lord of Hosts has spoken it.

Isaiah 5:20: Woe unto them that call evil good, and good evil; that put darkness for light, and light for darkness; that put bitter for sweet, and sweet for bitter!

Jeremiah 13:10: This evil people, which refuse to hear my words, which walk in the imagination of their heart, and walk after other gods, to serve them, and to worship them, shall even be as this girdle, which is good for nothing.

Matthew 5:7: Blessed are the merciful: for they shall obtain mercy.

5/17/12

CHANGE OF SEASONS

My people, you are in a change of seasons at this time. The old is giving way to the new, and at times it may feel strange to you. As I have told you before, do not try to take the old with you into the new, for there will be no place for it there.

I have spoken to many of you to clean up your lives—both spiritually and physically, including your environments. Many of you have obeyed Me, and more are obeying, and with you I am very pleased. Continue removing that which is no longer needed or useful to your spiritual walk with Me. You shall be very glad you have obeyed Me in this.

*As you clear out the old, consider how these things and people came to be in your lives, and learn from this lesson. **As you progress towards the end of time, there will be less and less room for anything or anyone in your lives that is not of Me.***

THE ENEMY OFTEN SENDS THINGS AND PEOPLE TO DISTRACT YOU FROM ME AND MY WORK, and you must be watchful at all times, for he has plans to increase these attacks on you in the very near future. Your diligence in these matters must be constantly increasing, IF YOU ARE TO SURVIVE WHAT IS COMING and complete the work I have for you.

Pray now for your loved ones to be strengthened to face the next phase of My plan, for you are rushing towards the end, and the time of earth as it is, is almost done.

Eccl. 3:1-3: To everything there is a season, and a time to every purpose under the heaven: A time to be born, and a time to die; a time to plant, and a time to pluck up that which is planted; A time to kill, and a time to heal; a time to break down, and a time to build up;

Eccl. 3:15-17: That which hath been is now; and that which is to be hath already been; and God requireth that which is past. And moreover I saw under the sun the place of judgment, that wickedness was there; and the place of righteousness, that iniquity was there. I said in mine heart, God shall judge the righteous and the wicked: for there is a time there for every purpose and for every work.

5/29/12

WILL YOU DENY ME?

Tell My children to prepare, for chaos lies ahead: in the near future, a time such as never before it, when chaos shall reign on the earth and orderliness and the law will seem a thing of the past. This shall strike fear in the hearts of many, but especially those who do not know Me.

I desire My children would trust in Me and remain in peace at that time, but it shall be a struggle for most.

Know that I am with you in all that is coming, My children. I walk alongside you in every battle, and we face every challenge together. You are never alone, though the enemy desires to make you think this is so. I will never leave you.

WILL YOU LEAVE ME in all that is to be? When the forces of Hell are turned out into the earth, will you deny Me and turn away, that you may feed your little ones? Or will you trust Me to feed them, and you?

WILL YOU LEAVE ME after all I have done for you in this life and the one to come?

WILL YOU DENY MY NAME in the time that is soon to come?

John 14:27: Peace I leave with you, my peace I give unto you: not as the world giveth, give I unto you. Let not your heart be troubled, neither let it be afraid.

Isaiah 26:3: Thou wilt keep him in perfect peace, whose mind is stayed on thee: because he trusteth in thee.

2 Timothy 1:7: For God hath not given us the spirit of fear; but of power, and of love, and of a sound mind.

Hebrews 13:5: Let your conversation be without covetousness; and be content with such things as ye have: for he hath said, I will never leave thee, nor forsake thee.

Psalm 37:18-20: The LORD knoweth the days of the upright: and their inheritance shall be for ever. They shall not be ashamed in the evil time: and in the days of famine they shall be satisfied. But the wicked shall perish, and the enemies of the LORD shall be as the fat of lambs: they shall consume; into smoke shall they consume away.

Matthew 10:33: But whosoever shall deny me before men, him will I also deny before my Father which is in heaven.

5/31/12

THE NEW AGE IS BEGINNING

My people, so many of you are completely unaware of the importance of the time you live in on the earth. All those in Heaven know and rejoice, yet so many of you go on with your day-to-day lives as though nothing had changed, when everything has changed.

The new age is beginning, and much will deteriorate from here. My glory will arise and shine on My appointed ones, those I have chosen to use in this time. Many shall reject the works they shall do, just as they rejected My Son, and they will be judged.

When He spoke this, I saw judgment falling quickly on those who mocked the End Times miracles.

Many shall reject the miracles they see, however great they are, and they <u>shall</u> be great. Many shall try to explain away My mighty power in that time, FOR I SHALL PERFORM FEATS NO MAN HAS EVER SEEN BEFORE. Miracles of a nature unbeknownst to man shall happen before your very eyes, My children, and many shall see and believe, in spite of those who mock.

You must walk carefully now before Me, little ones, for the enemy has set many new snares and traps for you, hoping to lure you away from My presence. He will succeed in luring some of you for a time and weaken you in this way.

I saw in the Spirit that this is the enemy's goal—to weaken us for further attack.

You must be strong in Me at all times if you are to survive what is coming in the near future. I have given you advance warning that you may prepare for all that lies ahead, for when it happens, it will happen all at once. Many seemingly simultaneous events will occur one after another after another. That is why there will be no time to prepare then.

Ready yourselves for My Son's soon return. Walk with Me in all your ways. Listen for My voice. Simplify your lives so that you may hear Me better. Be in My Word that I may speak to you there.

You live in a serious time, My children. Do not underestimate the power of the enemy of your souls. Be ever vigilant against his wiles. Watch and pray at all times, that you may finish your race with courage and conviction.

Isaiah 60:1-2: Arise, shine; for thy light is come, and the glory of the LORD is risen upon thee. For, behold, the darkness shall cover the earth, and gross darkness the people: but the LORD shall arise upon thee, and his glory shall be seen upon thee.

Isaiah 28:22: Now therefore be ye not mockers, lest your bands be made strong: for I have heard from the Lord GOD of hosts a consumption, even determined upon the whole earth.

Jude 1:8: How that they told you there should be mockers in the last time, who should walk after their own ungodly lusts.

1 Peter 5:8: Be sober, be vigilant; because your adversary the devil, as a roaring lion, walketh about, seeking whom he may devour:

Ephesians 6:11: Put on the whole armour of God, that ye may be able to stand against the wiles of the devil.

6/7/12

REGRET OR REWARD

I have spoken to you to leave behind the things of the past, yet many of you still cling to it. You cling to the people, the places, the things of the past that have no place in your future—in your future in Me. If you try to take the past into your future, you will find no place for it there, My people. There is no place in the chaos that is coming for your flesh.

Set your minds on Me and on the things of My Kingdom. Set your sights on your heavenly reward, for all that is now shall soon pass away. LIFE AS YOU KNOW IT WILL CEASE, but in My Kingdom, all things are made new.

You have asked Me for many things, and you have asked that I anoint you, yet you refuse to lay down the things I ask of you.

In the Spirit I saw the enemy handing us things to occupy us, much like a mother handing a small child a cheap toy to keep them busy and distracted so they won't fuss; while the Lord stands nearby, holding out to us a very genuine reward He wants to give to us. I saw that this is a very widespread attack of the enemy, trying to distract us from our walk with the Lord.

You are refusing to choose the things of Me when you cling to what is no longer useful, and many of you will be passed over for promotion because of this. I promote those who show themselves yielded vessels, ready for My use, obedient to My commands. I do not promote the disobedient.

Some of you have waited long for what is coming, yet have not made yourselves ready. Why must I continually speak this to you, My children? Why do you not obey as you know you should? Will you live lives of regret and not the rewards I have for you?

Some of you are obeying, and you shall be given much for your much obedience. Those who obey little shall be given little. Do not be deceived, children, I do not reward disobedience and sloppy living. I do not reward those who do not strive to walk in My ways. I do not reward those who do not honor My Son with their lives. You cannot serve two masters. Either you will serve your flesh, or you will serve Me, but you will not serve both and receive rewards from Me.

If you serve the enemy, then you receive his reward. If you serve Me—truly serve Me—you receive Mine. You cannot serve Me only with your lips; you must sacrifice the desires of your flesh, walk in My ways, be in My Word, do My will.

I try the heart and the reins, I know all things. I know the true motives behind your deeds, and I shall judge you accordingly.

The time to shake off the past is now, My children. Let go. Let go of the things of the flesh that no longer serve a useful purpose in your spiritual lives. Let go and come up higher with Me, for I have great rewards for you when you do.

Do not be deceived. You cannot serve the enemy and also serve Me, for He who is not for Me, is against Me.

Release the past.

Trust Me to meet your needs.

Luke 9:62: And Jesus said unto him, No man, having put his hand to the plough, and looking back, is fit for the kingdom of God.

2 Cor. 5:17: Therefore if any man be in Christ, he is a new creature: old things are passed away; behold, all things are become new.

2 Tim. 2:20-22: But in a great house there are not only vessels of gold and of silver, but also of wood and of earth; and some to honour, and some to dishonour. . If a man therefore purge himself from these, he shall be a vessel unto honour, sanctified, and meet for the master's use, and prepared unto every good work. Flee also youthful lusts: but follow righteousness, faith, charity, peace, with them that call on the Lord out of a pure heart.

Phil. 3:13-14: Brethren, I count not myself to have apprehended: but this one thing I do, forgetting those things which are behind, and reaching forth unto those things which are before, I press toward the mark for the prize of the high calling of God in Christ Jesus.

Jer. 17:10: I the LORD search the heart, I try the reins, even to give every man according to his ways, and according to the fruit of his doings.

Deut. 11:16: Take heed to yourselves, that your heart be not deceived, and ye turn aside, and serve other gods, and worship them;

Eph. 5:6: Let no man deceive you with vain words: for because of these things cometh the wrath of God upon the children of disobedience.

Gal. 6:7: Be not deceived; God is not mocked: for whatsoever a man soweth, that shall he also reap.

Matt. 15:8: This people draweth nigh unto me with their mouth, and honoureth me with their lips; but their heart is far from me.

6/15/12

SEEK WISDOM

The enemy seeks to destroy My people through old weaknesses, habits, and desires. He has drawn some of you back into sins you thought were long behind you. Sure you had overcome. You became less diligent, and he sought opportunity with you.

My people, do your eyes not see, and do you not understand why he does this at this time? Do you fail to perceive what is happening in your lives? Is your knowledge yet so dim that you are ignorant of his devices?

He comes to steal My Word from your hearts to sway you from walking in all My ways. He seeks to possess your gates, that he may come and go from your lives at will, and some of you are allowing him access.

Do you not know the outcome of this folly? If My Word is stolen from your hearts, there will be only darkness. You live in the time of separation. The dividing lines are being drawn; sides are being chosen. You vowed to fight for Me and with Me, yet you have chosen the ways of darkness.

He does this so when calamity strikes, you shall not be prepared, and will be taken with the others who do not serve Me or My Kingdom. In your hearts, you believe there will be time to repent for your sins, but for many of you there will not be. (At this point, I heard great sadness and grief in the Lord's voice.)

Many of you reading this shall indeed be taken very suddenly, without warning. You must be ready at all times, for this is a new time in the earth and things will change, and they will not change back, My children.

I have told you—you live in a time such as none before it. Many still refuse to see the lateness of the hour and shall perish in their folly, but My children—My chosen ones—should not be among those who live so foolishly.

Seek wisdom, My children. Seek wisdom before it is too late for you.

1 Peter 5:8: Be sober, be vigilant; because your adversary the devil, as a roaring lion, walketh about, seeking whom he may devour:

2 Cor. 2:11: Lest Satan should get an advantage of us: for we are not ignorant of his devices.

Acts 3:19: Repent ye therefore, and be converted, that your sins may be blotted out, when the times of refreshing shall come from the presence of the Lord.

Proverbs 1:25-27: But ye have set at nought all my counsel, and would none of my reproof: I also will laugh at your calamity; I will mock when your fear cometh; When your fear cometh as desolation, and your destruction cometh as a whirlwind; when distress and anguish cometh upon you.

Proverbs 5:22-23: His own iniquities shall take the wicked himself, and he shall be holden with the cords of his sins. He shall die without instruction; and in the greatness of his folly he shall go astray.

Proverbs 15:21: Folly is joy to him that is destitute of wisdom: but a man of understanding walketh uprightly.

Proverbs 1:7: The fear of the LORD is the beginning of knowledge: but fools despise wisdom and instruction.

6/21/12

AMERICA HAS BECOME A FESTERING WOUND

I was praying Wednesday evening, talking to the Lord about an article a friend had forwarded about someone being involuntarily committed to a mental hospital because of their belief in Christ. It struck me as a sign of things that are coming soon, and I began asking the Lord if He had any word for us this week. He spoke this to me.

Indeed hard times are coming soon, My child, to all the people of the earth, especially America. America has become a festering wound in My sight, her sin knows no bounds. She proudly and brazenly flaunts her evil ways for all the world to see without remorse. For this she shall be greatly punished.

My people who agree with her sinfulness shall know My judgment as well, for those who are truly Mine should not do so wickedly. Her sins have become a snare and like gods to you, My people. You prefer serving them, and your sinful desires, over serving Me, the Holy One of Israel. This should not be, and you shall pay a grave price for such wickedness.

I desire a pure and a holy people who serve Me with their whole hearts, but you have turned aside, and go whoring after other gods. You think I will not care, but you are mistaken, My children, for sin grieves Me, and arouses My holy anger when there is no repentance.

Will you serve Me or will you serve your flesh? You must choose, for the time of My judgments is at hand and I shall judge each house, and every person in it according to what I find there.

Hard times are coming for the people of the earth, but your sins will make them far harder than they would otherwise be for you.

Return to Me now while there is still time. Return to Me and cry out for forgiveness, that I may show you mercy, and your household. Cry out for your lost loved ones while there is yet time, for soon there will not be. Many shall be taken from you and not only you but they are also unprepared.

You weary yourselves with earthly preparations for earthly disasters, My people, but your concern should be for your spiritual state and that of your house, for I am a wealthy father and well able to provide for all your earthly needs in that time. Did I not say in My holy word Take no thought for tomorrow?

(Note: At this point, I asked the Lord about something He had said in earlier words, about storing up grain for our little ones, and He showed me here in this word He is speaking about people who are concerned about shelters and defenses, not food and water.)

Yet you are preoccupied with where you shall live and what you shall do.

Store up grain for your little ones and spend your time in My word that I may enlighten you more in what you must do, for surely you are not able to survive all that is to come without My guidance. Spend your hours in My presence and drawing near to Me, for that is what is truly needful in this hour.

Keep your eyes on Me, for I am your refuge. I am your strong tower. I will be your shelter in that time, in that hour. I am He who watches over you from above, who gives you breath and life and sustenance. You need not fear if you are truly Mine.

Isaiah 13:11: And I will punish the world for their evil, and the wicked for their iniquity; and I will cause the arrogancy of the proud to cease, and will lay low the haughtiness of the terrible.

Jeremiah 1:16: And I will utter my judgments against them touching all their wickedness, who have forsaken me, and have burned incense unto other gods, and worshipped the works of their own hands.

Joel 3:13: Put ye in the sickle, for the harvest is ripe: come, get you down; for the press is full, the fats overflow; for their wickedness is great.

Psalm 73:27: For, lo, they that are far from thee shall perish: thou hast destroyed all them that go a whoring from thee.

Isaiah 1:4: Ah sinful nation, a people laden with iniquity, a seed of evildoers, children that are corrupters: they have forsaken the LORD, they have provoked the Holy One of Israel unto anger, they are gone away backward.

Isaiah 55:7: Let the wicked forsake his way, and the unrighteous man his thoughts: and let him return unto the LORD, and he will have mercy upon him; and to our God, for he will abundantly pardon.

Matthew 6:34: Take therefore no thought for the morrow: for the morrow shall take thought for the things of itself. Sufficient unto the day is the evil thereof.

Psalm 46:1: God is our refuge and strength, a very present help in trouble.

Psalm 91:2: I will say of the LORD, He is my refuge and my fortress: my God; in him will I trust.

Psalm 61:3: For thou hast been a shelter for me, and a strong tower from the enemy.

Proverbs 18:10: The name of the LORD is a strong tower: the righteous runneth into it, and is safe.

Job 12:10: In whose hand is the soul of every living thing, and the breath of all mankind.

6/22/12

I DESIRE YOUR LOVE

Tell My people, child. Not spending time in worship to Me is very serious and grievous in My sight. I desire My people's presence.

I desire your love, My people. I desire you would come into My presence and lavish Me with your love and adoration, for then do our spirits commune as one. Then are you truly acting as My bride.

I desire your presence. I desire to feel your love and hear your words of adoration to Me. I desire you, that is why I created you to worship Me!

Yes, I am Almighty God. I am the great Jehovah God to whom nothing is impossible and you who worship Me in spirit and in truth are truly My people. Those who go about their days to whom I am an afterthought are serving Me with their lips only and their prayers I will not honor.

It is those whose hearts I truly reign in who truly know Me, and who I know. These draw near to Me daily. These are those on whom My glory and fiery power shall fall in days coming. These shall I protect and preserve.

Those of you who ignore Me while you pursue earthly pleasures commit a grave error, for you shall not be able to enter into My presence when tragedy falls around you, though you shall long to.

If you seek Me now, you shall find Me. Those who wait will walk a far more difficult path. You shall long for My presence and not find it. You shall desire to hear My voice and hear it not.

Build your house on the rock, My children. On the rock of My love, My presence, My Son, My Word, and all that I am, and you shall be safe, but you cannot have part of Me - you must take all. Come into My presence and learn of Me.

I desire your love and worship. I am a holy God. You must obey Me in all things if I am to be your God. Come to Me now before it is too late for you

Deut. 4:29: But if from thence thou shalt seek the LORD thy God, thou shalt find him, if thou seek him with all thy heart and with all thy soul.

Matthew 7:7-8: Ask, and it shall be given you; seek, and ye shall find; knock, and it shall be opened unto you: For every one that asketh receiveth; and he that seeketh findeth; and to him that knocketh it shall be opened.

Psalm 31:2: Bow down thine ear to me; deliver me speedily: be thou my strong rock, for an house of defence to save me.

Matthew 7:24: And the rain descended, and the floods came, and the winds blew, and beat upon that house; and it fell not: for it was founded upon a rock.

Isaiah 58:2: Yet they seek me daily, and delight to know my ways, as a nation that did righteousness, and forsook not the ordinance of their God: they ask of me the ordinances of justice; they take delight in approaching to God.

6/26/12

I AM HE WHO DELIVERS

I am able to help My people regardless of what befalls them in the future. The enemy shall indeed set many traps and snares for you, My children, but I am He who delivers from all things not of Me.

I am He who no man and no evil can stand before, for I am holy and righteous and there is none other like Me.

Fear not, little flock, for I am well able to protect you in what is coming. For those of you who fall into snares, I am able to set you free with a word. I am well able to do all My good pleasure in your life and there is none like Me, no, not in all of heaven or earth. There is no other who can deliver and none can deliver out of My hand.

Deut. 3:24: O Lord GOD, thou hast begun to shew thy servant thy greatness, and thy mighty hand: for what God is there in heaven or in earth, that can do according to thy works, and according to thy might?

Deut. 4:35: Unto thee it was shewed, that thou mightest know that the LORD he is God; there is none else beside him.

1Kings 8:23: And he said, LORD God of Israel, there is no God like thee, in heaven above, or on earth beneath, who keepest covenant and mercy with thy servants that walk before thee with all their heart:

2 Samuel 7:22: Wherefore thou art great, O LORD God: for there is none like thee, neither is there any God beside thee, according to all that we have heard with our ears.

Daniel 3:17: If it be so, our God whom we serve is able to deliver us from the burning fiery furnace, and he will deliver us out of thine hand, O king.

Isaiah 43:13: Yea, before the day was I am he; and there is none that can deliver out of my hand: I will work, and who shall let it?

Isaiah 41:10: Fear thou not; for I am with thee: be not dismayed; for I am thy God: I will strengthen thee; yea, I will help thee; yea, I will uphold thee with the right hand of my righteousness.

7/05/12

FORTIFY YOURSELVES

Events are heating up on the world scene, My children, and conditions are about to get very bad in some areas. (I saw He meant some areas of the world) Hold on to your faith in Me, no matter what you see transpiring around you, for nothing matters in the end if you fail to keep that.

I will be speaking to some of you soon about ministries you are to begin doing. I wish My gospel to be preached to the lost, that they be given one more chance to repent while there is yet time.

Time is quickly running out and there is no time for turning back or turning away from Me. You must guard your hearts with all diligence, for much of what you see will incite fear in you, and you shall be tempted to stop believing in Me. The enemy will try to make the most of this. When this happens, remind yourselves of all that was foretold in My Holy Word, and realize what you are seeing is simply the fulfillment of My promises about the end.

Those who endure, believing, will be greatly rewarded. You have been chosen to live in this time, My children. Only the very strongest can survive in what is coming. The strongest in Me, not in yourselves. Fortify yourselves in My Holy Word and get ready to do battle.

Be armed and ready to do battle in your houses against the evil that is coming for you. Be ready to battle the onslaught of temptations the enemy is launching on you. Realize he desires to weaken you by getting you off track. As he distracts you, he steals My Word from your hearts and minds and renders you unprepared to fight his next attack on you, on your household.

Get ready to do battle in your cities, for every city in every nation will be attacked by the enemy's forces in this time. Those evidencing My glory will be hardest hit. He will show no mercy, My children, but those of you who prepare by soaking up My Word, by knowing Me, by sitting in My presence daily, and seeking Me, shall walk through this time unafraid and I shall use you to do mighty exploits among your brethren. Unbelievers will watch in awe at My mighty power evidenced through you as I perform feats never before witnessed on earth.

The time of My glory has come. Do not waste it being fearful or distracted. Use it. Use it to witness of My greatness, My great power and majesty in the earth, that more souls may come into My Kingdom.

Hebrews 10:23: Let us hold fast the profession of our faith without wavering; (for he is faithful that promised;)

Mark 16:15: And he said unto them, Go ye into all the world, and preach the gospel to every creature.

Proverbs 4:23: Keep thy heart with all diligence; for out of it are the issues of life.

James 1:12: Blessed is the man that endureth temptation: for when he is tried, he shall receive the crown of life, which the Lord hath promised to them that love him.

Matthew 10:22: And ye shall be hated of all men for my name's sake: but he that endureth to the end shall be saved.

1 Peter 5:8: Be sober, be vigilant; because your adversary the devil, as a roaring lion, walketh about, seeking whom he may devour:

2 Timothy 1:7: For God hath not given us the spirit of fear; but of power, and of love, and of a sound mind.

EPILOGUE

There are many who claim God no longer speaks to His people, but Jesus said in John 10:27, *My sheep hear My voice, and I know them, and they follow me*. In order for His sheep to hear His voice, He must be speaking. To say He does not speak to His people, when He clearly spoke all the way from Genesis to Revelations because you have never heard Him speak, is not only not scriptural, but it is highly presumptuous.

These attitudes may be partly a result of some simply not being able to understand what they have not seen or experienced. Clearly there are many things that are not part of our personal experience, but that does not make them irrelevant, evil, or delusional.

God is the same yesterday, today and forever, and He has much to say to a people He created to be in relationship with. The real question is, how many are listening?

I prayed for some time about publishing this book, having received numerous requests to compile the prophecies from the

Wings of Prophecy website into hard copy format, but knowing it would most likely draw a mixed reaction. Even as I prayed about it, I was personally against doing it until the Lord spoke to me in May of 2012. This is what He said.

I will bless the word book that My words may reach My people. You will indeed receive much criticism for this book, but ignore them, for this is truly My will for you to do. I have My prophets write My words today just as I did in days of old and many refuse to hear My words, just as they did then. It will be well received by those with ears to hear and that is who it is for. Ignore the others.

In that moment I understood it truly was His will that this book be completed.

The other reason I held back from compiling it was because of multiple projects already in the works. I wasn't sure where I could find the time to work on anything more than what I had already begun. As always, though, when the Lord gives you an assignment, He is faithful to send qualified people to help you.

When my good friend, Rudy Schafer, offered to contribute his own time in order to make the book happen, I knew it was another confirmation from the Lord that He wanted the book being published. Were it not for Rudy's selfless giving to this project, I don't know when the book would actually have ended up being available. I thank God for brothers and sisters like Rudy in the Body of Christ who give so willingly into His work, that others may benefit.

It is my prayer that these words will help you draw nearer to the King of Kings, in preparation for all He desires to do in your life, and all that is coming in the future. May it enrich your life and your walk in every possible way.

God bless you,

Glynda Lomax

P.O. Box 127
Princeton, Texas 75407
www.wingsofprophecy.com

WEBSITES

Wings of Prophecy Site:
http://www.wingsofprophecy.com

Listen to Wings Radio on Blog Talk Radio:
http://www.blogtalkradio.com/glyndalomax

My YouTube Channel:
http://www.youtube.com/user/texasauthor1

Other Books by Glynda Lomax:

The Wilderness Companion

CROSS REFERENCE INDEX BY SUBJECT

America

A Sad Time Is Approaching...149

America, America...194

America Has Become A Festering Wound...204

America Has Become the Harlot of the World...75

America Shall Bow...99

America Will Suffer Many Wounds...45

Destruction Is Coming to America...72

Great Saving, Healing, Delivering...29

It Is Time to Choose...93

Prepare Your Hearts...116

She Has Turned Against Me...151

So It Will Be for Every Nation That Forgets Me...129

The Coming Attack on America...4

The Enemy Has Lulled You To Sleep..113

The Enemy Will Pursue My People...9

There Shall Be Weeping and Mourning In America...81

There Will Be An Increase In My Words...33

This Is the Calm Before the Storm...39

Visions of Famine Coming to America...2

Weep for America....5

Angels

Give to the People On the Streets...17

Situations Are Not As They Appear To Be...63

The Great Warriors...12

The Time Has Come To Promote My People...155

This Storm Will Come Upon Your Quickly...66

This Year...178

You Must Now Constantly Seek My Face...120

Battle/Soldiers/Warriors/War

A Year of Much Change...46

Cry Out to Me...119

Fortify Yourselves...210

I Am Calling My Soldiers to War...114

I Am Coming to Every Household...111

I Am Stirring Up Nations...173

I Will Not Look the Other Way...123

Prepare for War...187

Rise Up and Fight the Enemy...95

The Great Warriors...12

The Time Has Come To Promote My People...155

The Time of My Great Warriors...50

What's Coming in 2011...19

Will You Deny Me?...196

You Have Heard the Warning Sound...55

Behind the Scenes/Change Coming

Be Vigilant...136

Draw Near to Me...115

Obey Me Now...42

Situations Are Not As They Appear To Be...63

So It Will Be For Every Nation That Forgets Me...129

When Will You Heed My Words?...77

Bride/Marriage Feast

Chained...192

Draw Near To Me Now...102

False Shepherds Will Lose Their Flocks...12

Hard Times Lie Ahead...110

My Bride Is Indifferent to Me...103

My Chosen Ones...38

Only One...132

Situations Are Not As They Appear To Be...63

The Great Warriors...12

They Have Worshiped Other Gods...11

This Is the Calm Before the Storm...39

Vision of the Wounded Lambs...163

What's Coming in 2011...19

Darkness/Time of Darkness

Be Vigilant...136

Draw Near To Me Now...102

Great Change Is Coming - Trust Me...22

Situations Are Not As They Appear To Be...63

The Days Grow Darker Still...138

The Enemy Will Pursue My People...9

The Meat Grinder Vision...175

There Shall Be Weeping and Mourning in America...81

They Have Worshiped Other Gods...11

You Have Heard the Warning Sound...55

Destruction/Events/Storms Coming

A Throwaway God...177

A Time of Many Dangers...31

An Event Is Coming Soon That Will Shock the World...27

Cry Out to Me...119

Destruction Is Coming to America...72

I Am Calling My Soldiers to War...114

I Am Coming to Every Household...111

I Delight In Your True Worship of Me...100

It Is Time to Choose...93

It Is Time...145

It Will Be A Time As None Before It...117

Only One...132

Prepare Your Hearts...116

Rise Up and Fight the Enemy...95

The Days Grow Darker Still...138

The Enemy Has Lulled You To Sleep...113

The Enemy Will Pursue My People...9

The Shaking Is Beginning...184

The Time Has Come To Promote My People...155

The Time of My Great Warriors...50

The Time of My Judgments Has Come...124

The Time of Shaking Is Upon You...153

There Will Be An Increase In My Words...33

This Storm Will Come Upon Your Quickly...66

Trouble Coming...60

Unions Not of Me...183

When Will You Heed My Words?...77

Will You Deny Me?...196

Evil One/Man of Perdition/Evil

A Sad Time Is Approaching...149

As You Have Sown, So Shall You Reap...34

Chained...192

Draw Near to Me...115

Great Changes...143

It Is Time to Choose...93

It Is Time...145

Rend Your Hearts to Me...91

Rise Up and Fight the Enemy...95

They Shall Be Deceived...147

When Will You Heed My Words?...77

Which Is More Important?...157

Why Do You Not Worship Me?...97

Why Do You Say You Are Mine?...89

You Are To Be That Light...158

False Shepherds/Priests/Corrupt Church

2012 - Many Change, Miracles...160

A Great Saving, Healing, Delivering...29

A Year of Much Change...46

False Shepherds Will Lose Their Flocks...12

Want of Gain...181

What's Coming in 2011...19

Weep for America...5

You Must Forgive...108

Famine/Storing up Food/Preparing

A Year of Much Change...46

America Has Become A Festering Wound...204

America Shall Bow...99

An Event Is Coming Soon That Will Shock the World...27

Cry Out to Me...119

Hard Times Lie Ahead...110

I Am Raising Up Some of You to Lead...84

I Desire That My People Would Prepare...77

The Time of My Great Warriors...50

There Shall Be Weeping and Mourning in America...81

Trouble Coming...60

Visions of Famine Coming to America...2

Weep for America...5

Why Do You Say You Are Mine?...89

Why Is Your Faith So Small?...131

Intercession/Interceding for the Lost

2012 - Many Change, Miracles...160

America Has Become A Festering Wound...204

Change of Seasons...195

Cry Out to Me for Your Lost Loved Ones...16

His Attacks Have Increased...152

I Am Calling My Soldiers to War...114

The Enemy Will Pursue My People...9

They Shall Be Deceived...147

This Year...178

Which Is More Important?...157

You Must Now Constantly Seek My Face...120

Judgment/Sin

A Sad Time Is Approaching...149

A Time of Many Transitions...189

A Throwaway God...177

A Year of Much Change...46

America, America...194

America Has Become A Festering Wound...204

America Has Become the Harlot of the World...75

America Shall Bow...99

America Will Suffer Many Wounds...45

As You Have Sown, So Shall You Now Reap...34

Change Is Coming...140

Cry Out to Me...119

Destruction Is Coming to America...72

Hard Times Lie Ahead...110

I Am Coming to Every Household...111

It Is Time to Choose...93

Obey Me Now...42

Prepare for War...187

Prepare Your Hearts...116

Repent While There Is Still Time...86

Seek Me For I Shall Be Found...169

She Has Turned Against Me...151

So It Will Be For Every Nation That Forgets Me...129

The Blanket of Darkness...1

The Enemy Has Lulled You To Sleep...113

The Enemy Will Pursue My People...9

The New Age Is Beginning...197

The Time of My Judgments Has Come...124

The Time of Shaking Is Upon You...153

There Shall Be Weeping and Mourning in America...81

This Shall Be A Year of Turning...125

Those Who Do Not Make Time for God Now...8

Trouble Coming...60

Want of Gain...181

Weep for America...5

What's Coming in 2011...19

You Cannot Love the World and Love Me...69

You Must Now Constantly Seek My Face...120

You Must Forgive...108

Miracles, Signs and Wonders

2012 - Many Change, Miracles...160

A Great Saving, Healing, Delivering...29

Destruction Is Coming to America...72

Draw Near to Me...115

I Will Shower Them In the Miraculous...106

Obey Me Now...42

Rend Your Hearts to Me...91

The New Age Is Beginning...197

They Shall Be Ashamed...25

This Year...178

Trouble Coming...60

Why Is Your Faith So Small?...131

You Must Now Constantly Seek My Face...120

Worship

A Year of Much Change...46

Awesome Worship?...16

I Delight In Your True Worship of Me...100

I Desire Your Love...207

I Will Shower Them In the Miraculous...106

My People Must Take Control of Their Mouths...122

This Year...178

Why Do You Not Worship Me?..97

NOTES

Made in the USA
Charleston, SC
18 July 2012